There likely has never been a more attractive and yet definitive exposition of the Gospel message answering the age-old question offered by Job—How can a man be right with God? Horatius Bonar's Gospel primer provides for us an incomparable instrument for personal growth, evangelism and discipleship.

HARRY L. REEDER, III
Senior Pastor, Briarwood Presbyterian Church, Birmingham, Alabama

This book is for sinners—sinners, whether Christians or not, who are troubled by their sin and want to know how they can have lasting peace in mind, heart and conscience. Horatius Bonar is a safe guide. He explains clearly and patiently all that God has done in Jesus Christ to save sinners from the guilt and power of their sin and grant to them eternal life. With urgency, yet with great kindness, Bonar directs us to the finished work of the crucified Christ as the only sure way of peace. This book is an invaluable comfort to troubled consciences of all kinds.

ROBERT STRIVENS
Pastor, Bradford on Avon Baptist Church, Bradford on Avon

God's Way of Peace

Overcoming Anxiety by Walking with God

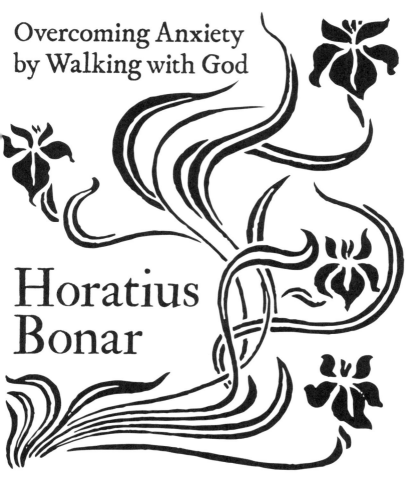

Horatius Bonar

Foreword by Matt Boswell

CHRISTIAN
HERITAGE

Scripture quotations are based on the *King James Version*.

Copyright © Christian Focus Publications 2021

ISBN 978-1-5271-0609-3

Published in 2021
by
Christian Focus Publications Ltd,
Geanies House, Fearn, Ross-shire
IV20 1TW, Scotland
www.christianfocus.com

Cover design by Daniel Van Straaten

The Fell Types are digitally reproduced
by Igino Marini. www.iginomarini.com

Printed and bound by Gutenberg

CONTENTS

FOREWORD

The first sermon Horatius Bonar (1808–1889) preached as the minister at the North Parish Church in Kelso, Scotland, demonstrates the urgency he felt regarding the salvation of the men and women he was called to serve as pastor. He began his ministry confessing:

> My dear brethren, I do not come to address you after the manner of man's wisdom, nor with words of human eloquence, but to speak to your souls of the things which concern your eternity—to stir you up to see in good earnest salvation for yourselves and for others.[1]

The fervor conveyed in these opening remarks saturate *God's Way of Peace.* The question of whether or not we have peace with God is a matter of eternal significance. Bonar speaks passionately and clearly to anxious hearts who

---

1   *Horatius Bonar, D. D., A Memorial* (New York: Robert Carter & Bros., 1889), 61.

lack peace with God. With each chapter he administers the only remedy for the sin-sick soul: the gospel of Jesus Christ. My prayer is that you would give this book your full attention, whether you are filled with anxiety over your sin or you are simply indifferent. There is no greater peace than knowing God.

A Snapshot Biography

Horatius Bonar was a Scottish pastor, author, and hymnwriter who sought to serve God and His church with his life and ministry. Bonar was licensed in 1833, and after pastoring in Leith for four years, was installed as minister of the North Parish Church in Kelso, where he ministered for twenty-nine years. Bonar was committed to preaching the gospel of Jesus Christ from the Scriptures, and passionately exposited texts unfolding God's truth for His people. As a part of his desire to see people come to know Jesus Christ and to grow in their faith, he began his writing endeavors. Initially, Bonar wrote short tracts— known as the 'Kelso Tracts'—as a means of evangelism and discipleship. Later, he published a number of books to help people know and grow in the faith once for all delivered to the saints. Bonar also wrote poems and hymns to accompany the rich doctrinal truths he held so dear. Bonar regularly published hymns from 1844 to 1881, his greatest contribution being the hymnal *Hymns of Faith and Hope*, which eventually spanned three volumes. As an extension of his pastoral ministry, Bonar is regarded as the finest Scottish hymn-writer of the nineteenth century.[2] John Julian (1839–1913) said that Bonar's hymns 'mirror the life of Christ in the soul, partially, perhaps, but with vivid accuracy; they win the heart by their tone of tender sympathy; they sing the truth of God in ringing notes.'[3] In the final few years of his life, Bonar became the first minister of Chalmers Memorial Church in Edinburgh. He died on July 31, 1889.

GOD'S WAY OF PEACE

God's Way of Peace is one of the most compelling and patient presentations of the gospel of Jesus Christ I have ever read. In the pages that lie before you, Bonar presents a gospel primer full of the beauty and sufficiency of what Christ has done in order to bring peace to sinners. With each lesson he teaches us the remarkable basic truths of our faith and lays a foundation of salvation by faith alone through grace alone in Christ alone. Bonar is both bold and compassionate in his presentation. He wants us to see the truth of the gospel: that Jesus died in the place of ruined sinners, so that we might become the heirs of grace.

Christians would do well to rehearse their own salvation as Bonar leads them to remember their journey of passing from death to life in Christ. I pray that each believer who opens this book would gain deeper understanding of the gospel of

---

2 Michael A. G. Haykin, foreword to *Night of Weeping, Morning of Joy*, by Horatius Bonar (Grand Rapids: Reformation Heritage, 2008), 8.

3 John Julian, *A Dictionary of Hymnology: Setting Forth the Origin of Christian Hymns of All Ages and Nations* (J. Murray, 1892), 161.

peace, and might reach the end worshiping the God of our Salvation. I pray that for many who read these pages who have not yet believed upon the Lord Jesus as the only way to true and eternal peace with God, that you would come to see that the only way to peace with God is through the blood of Jesus that was shed. O, reader, believe the good news of this gospel! This work's subtitle calls to the anxious, but the anxiety it deals with is deeper than the fleeting burdens of this life; it is written to those who are anxious concerning their standing before God because of their sin.

The hymns written by Dr. Bonar contain many selections that would pair well with this book, however, 'The Voice from Galilee' seems to best carry the theme. Bonar opens the hymn with a testimonial reflection of when he first heard the call of Christ to come just as he was, and by believing in Christ he found a resting place for his soul (Matt. 11:28). Verse 2 recalls how he heard the invitation of Christ, given to everyone who thirsts, to come and find forgiveness and peace with God (John 7). The final verse acknowledges that Christ is the only light strong enough to flood our darkness and to illuminate our path (John 8:12). The verses may tell of Bonar's own personal experience of salvation, but they also tell the story of each of us who have come to trust in Christ as Savior. In this work and this hymn, Bonar beckons to those who have yet to trust in Jesus, that they might call upon Him and find peace for their anxious souls.

Matthew Boswell
Celina, Texas
July 2020

THE VOICE FROM GALILEE

I heard the voice of Jesus say,
Come unto Me and rest;
Lay down, thou weary one, lay down
Thy head upon My breast.
I came to Jesus as I was,
Weary, and worn, and sad,
I found in Him a resting-place,
And He has made me glad.

I heard the voice of Jesus say,
Behold, I freely give
The living water—thirsty one,
Stoop down, and drink, and live.
I came to Jesus, and I drank
Of that life-giving stream,
My thirst was quenched, my soul revived,
And now I live in Him.

I heard the voice of Jesus say,
I am this dark world's light,
Look unto Me, thy morn shall rise
And all thy day be bright.
I looked to Jesus, and I found
In Him, my Star, my Sun;
And in that Light of life I'll walk,
Till traveling days are done.

Horatius Bonar, 1857

Preface

'Therefore being justified by faith, we have peace with God through our Lord Jesus Christ.'—Romans 5:1

There seem to be many in our day who are seeking God. Yet they appear to be but feeling 'after Him', in order to 'find Him', as if He were either a distant or an 'unknown God'. They forget that He is *'not far* from every one of us', for 'in him we live, and move, and have our being' (Acts 17:23, 27-28).

That He is not far, that He has come down, that He has come near—this is the 'beginning of the gospel' (Mark 1:1). It sets aside the vain thoughts of those who think that they must bring Him near by their prayers and devout performances. He has shown Himself to us that we may know Him, and in knowing Him find the life of our souls.

With some who call themselves Christians, religion is a very unfinished thing. It drags heavily and is not satisfactory, either to the religious performers of it or the onlookers. There is no substance in it and no comfort. There is earnestness perhaps, but there is no 'peace with God' (Rom. 5:1), and so there is not even the root or foundation of that which God calls 'religion'. It needs to begin over again.

Acceptance with God lies at the foundation of all religion, for there must be an accepted worshipper before there can be acceptable worship. Religion is, with many, merely the means of averting God's displeasure and securing His favour. It is often irksome, but they do not feel easy in neglecting it; and they hope that by it they may obtain forgiveness before they die.

This, however, is the inversion of God's order, and is in reality the worship of an unknown God. It terminates in forgiveness; whereas God's religion begins with it. All false religions, though outwardly differing very widely, are made up of earnest efforts to secure for the religionists the divine favour now, and eternal life at last. The one true religion is seen in the holy life of those who, having found for themselves forgiveness and favour in believing the record that God has given of His Son, are *walking with Him* from day to day in the calm but sure consciousness of being entirely accepted, and *working for Him* with the happy earnestness of those whose reward is His constant smile of love. [These], having been much forgiven, love much and show, by daily sacrifice and service, how much they feel themselves debtors to a redeeming God, debtors to His Church, and debtors to the world in which they live (Rom. 1:14).

But if this be true religion, how much is there of the false? It is not good that men should be all their life seeking God and never finding Him, that they should be 'ever learning, and never able to come to the knowledge of the truth' (2 Tim. 3:7). It is not good to be always doubting—and when challenged, to make the untrue excuse that they are only doubting themselves, not God; that they are only dissatisfied with their own faith, but not with its glorious object. It is not good to believe in our own faith, still less in our own doubts, as some seem to do, making the best doubter to be the best believer—as if it were the gold of the cup, not the living water which it contains, that was to quench our thirst; and as if it were unlawful to take that precious water from a poor earthen vessel, such as our imperfect faith must ever be!

In this momentous thing, surely it is with the water, and not with the vessel, that the thirsty soul has to do! It is not the quality of the vessel, but the quality of the water, that the thirsty soul thinks of. He, whose pride will not allow him to drink out of a soiled or broken pitcher, must die of thirst. So he who puts away the sure reconciliation of the cross because of an imperfect faith, must die the death. He who says, 'I believe the right thing, but I don't believe it in the right way, and therefore I can't have peace', is the man whose pride is such that he is determined not to quench his thirst save out of a cup of gold!

Some have tried to give directions to sinners [about] 'how to get converted', multiplying words without wisdom (Job 35:16), leading the sinner away from the cross by setting him upon *doing*, not upon *believing*. Our business is not to give any such directions, but, as the apostles did, to preach Christ crucified, a present Saviour and a present salvation. Then it is that sinners are converted, as the Lord Himself said, 'I, if I be lifted up...will draw all men unto me' (John 12:32).

In the following chapters, there are some things that may appear repetitious. But this could not easily be avoided, as there were certain truths, as well as certain errors, that necessarily came up at different points and under different aspects. I need not apologize for these, as they were, in a great measure, unavoidable. They take up very little space, and I do not think they will seem at all superfluous to anyone who reads for profit and not for criticism.

Horatius Bonar

I

GOD'S TESTIMONY CONCERNING MAN

God knows us. He knows what we are; He knows also what He meant us to be. Upon the difference between these two states, He founds His testimony concerning us.

He is too loving to say anything needlessly severe; too true to say anything untrue. Nor can He have any motive to misrepresent us; for He loves to tell of the good, not of the evil, that may be found in any of the works of His hands. He declared them good, 'very good', at first (Gen. 1:31); and if He does not do so now, it is not because He would not, but because He cannot; for 'all flesh has corrupted its way upon the earth' (Gen. 6:12).

The divine testimony concerning man is that he is a *sinner*. God bears witness against him, not for him. [God] testifies that 'there is none righteous, no, not one'; that there is 'none that doeth good'; none 'that understandeth'; none that even seeks after God, and still more, none that loves Him (Ps. 14:1-3; Rom. 3:10-12). God speaks of man kindly, but severely; as one yearning over a lost child, yet as one who will make no terms with sin, and will 'by no means clear the guilty' (Exod. 34:7). He declares man to be a lost one, a stray one, a rebel, a *'hater of God '* (Rom. 1:30)—not a sinner occasionally, but a sinner always; not a sinner in part, with many good things about him; but wholly a sinner, with no compensating goodness; evil in heart as well as life, 'dead in trespasses and sins' (Eph. 2:1); an evil doer and therefore under condemnation; an enemy of God and therefore under wrath (James 4:4); a breaker of the righteous Law and therefore under 'the curse of the law' (Gal. 3:10).

Man has fallen! Not this man or that man, but the whole race! In Adam all have sinned; in Adam all have died (Rom. 3:23; 1 Cor. 15:22). It is not that a few leaves have faded or been shaken down, but the tree has become corrupt, root and branch. The 'flesh', or 'old man'—that is, each man as he is born into the world, a son of man, a fragment of humanity, a unit in Adam's fallen body—is 'corrupt' (Gen. 6:12). The sinner not merely brings forth sin, but he carries it about with him as his second self; he is a 'body' or mass of sin (Rom. 6:6), a 'body of death' (Rom. 7:24), subject not to the Law of God but to 'the law of sin' (Rom. 7:23). The Jew, educated under the most perfect of laws and in the most favourable circumstances, was the best type of humanity, of civilized, polished, educated humanity; the best specimen of Adam's sons—yet God's testimony concerning him is that he is 'under sin', that he has gone astray, and that he has 'come short of the glory of God' (Rom. 3:9, 23).

The outer life of a man is not the man, just as the paint on a piece of timber is not the timber, and as the green moss upon the hard rock is not the rock itself. The picture of a man is not the man; it is but a skillful arrangement of colours that look like the man. So it is the bearing of the soul toward God that is the true state of the man. The man that loves God with all his heart is in a right state; the man that does not love Him thus is in a wrong one—he is a sinner, because his heart is not right with God. He may think his life a good one, and others may think the same; but God counts him guilty, worthy of death and hell. The outward good cannot make up for the inward evil. The good deeds done to his fellow-men cannot be set off against his bad thoughts of God. And he must be full of these bad thoughts, so long as he does not love this infinitely lovable and infinitely glorious Being with all his strength.

God's testimony then concerning man is that he does not love God with all his heart; indeed, that he does not love Him at all. Not to love our neighbour is sin; not to love a parent is greater sin; but not to love God is greater sin still (Mark 12:33).

Man need not try to say a good word for himself or to plead 'not guilty', unless he can show that he loves, and has always loved, God with his whole heart and soul (Deut. 6:5). If he can truly say this, he is all right; he is not a sinner and does not need pardon. He will find his way to the kingdom without the cross and without a Saviour!

But if he cannot say this, his 'mouth' is 'stopped', and he is 'guilty before God' (Rom. 3:19). However favourably a good outward life may dispose him and others to look upon his case just now, the verdict will go against him hereafter. This is man's day, when man's judgments prevail; but God's day is coming, when the case shall be tried upon its real merits. Then the Judge of all the earth shall do right (Gen. 18:25), and the sinner be put to shame.

There is another and yet worse charge against him: he does not believe on the name of the Son of God, nor love the Christ of God. This is his sin of sins. That his heart is not right with God is the first charge against him. That his heart is not right with the Son of God is the second. And it is this second that is the crowning, crushing sin, carrying with it more terrible damnation than all other sins together. 'He that believeth not is condemned already, *because he hath not believed* in the name of the only begotten Son of God' (John 3:18). 'He that believeth not God hath made him a liar; *because he believeth not* the record that God gave of his Son' (1 John 5:10). 'He that *believeth not* shall be damned' (Mark 16:16). And hence it is that the first sin which the Holy Spirit brings home to a man is *unbelief*; 'when he [the Holy Spirit] is come, he will reprove the world of sin...*because they believe not* on me' (John 16:8-9).

Such is God's condemnation of man. Of this the whole Bible is full. That great love of God, which His Word reveals, is based on this condemnation. It is love to the condemned! God's testimony to His own grace has no meaning, save as resting on, or taking for granted His testimony to man's guilt and ruin. Nor is it against man as merely being morally diseased or sadly unfortunate that He testifies, but as guilty of death, under wrath, sentenced to the eternal curse—for that crime of crimes: a heart not right with God and not true to His incarnate Son.

This is a divine verdict, not a human one. It is God, not man, who condemns, and 'God is not a man, that he should lie' (Num. 23:19). This is God's testimony concerning man, and we know that this witness is true. It concerns us much to receive it as such, and act upon it!

2

Man's Own Character No Ground of Peace

If God testifies against us, who can testify *for* us? If God's opinion of man's sinfulness, His judgment of man's guilt, and His declaration of sin's evil be so very decided, there can be no hope of acquittal for us on the ground of personal character or goodness, either of heart or life. That which God sees in us furnishes only matter for condemnation, not for pardon.

It is vain to struggle or murmur against God's judgment. He is the Judge of all the earth; and He is right as well as sovereign in His judgment. He must be obeyed; His Law is inexorable; it cannot be broken without making the breaker of it (even in one jot or tittle) worthy of death.

When the Holy Spirit opens the eyes of the soul, it sees this. Conviction of sin is just the sinner seeing himself as he is and as God has all along seen him. Then every fond idea of self-goodness, either in whole or in part, vanishes away. The things in him that once seemed good appear so bad, and the bad things so very bad, that every self-prop falls from beneath him, and all hope of being saved, in consequence of something in his own character, is then taken away. He sees that he cannot save himself, nor help God to save him. He is *lost*, and he is *helpless*. Doings, feelings, strivings, prayings, givings, abstainings, and the like, are found to be no relief from a sense of guilt and, therefore, no resting place for a troubled heart. If sin were but a disease or a misfortune, these apparent good things might relieve him, as being favourable symptoms of returning health; but when sin is guilt even more than disease, and when the sinner is not merely sick but condemned by the righteous Judge, then none of these goodnesses, whether inner or outer, can reach his case—for they cannot assure him of a complete and righteous pardon and, therefore, cannot pacify his roused and wounded conscience. He sees God's unchangeable hatred of sin and the coming revelation of His wrath against the sinner, and he cannot but tremble.

The question, 'Wherewith shall I come before the Lord?' is not one which can be decided by an appeal to personal character or goodness of life, to prayers, or to performances of religion. The way of approach is not for us to settle. God has settled it, and it only remains for us to avail ourselves of it. He has fixed it on grounds altogether irrespective of our character; or rather, on grounds which take for granted simply that we are sinners, and that therefore the element of goodness in us—as a title, warrant, or recommendation—is altogether inadmissible, either in whole or in part.

Man is bankrupt, totally so; his credit in the market is gone. If, then, he is to carry on his trade, he cannot do it in his own name. He must have a better name than that, a name of note and weight, for his security. For the transactions of the heavenly market, there is but one name given under heaven, the Name of names!

To say, as some do at the outset of their anxiety, 'I will set myself to pray, and after I have prayed a sufficient length of time, and with tolerable earnestness, I may approach and count upon acceptance', is not only to build upon the quality and quantity of our prayers, but it is to overlook the real question before the sinner, 'How am I to approach God in order to pray?' All prayers are approaches to God, and the sinner's anxious question is, 'How may I approach God?' God's explicit testimony to man is, 'You are unfit to approach Me'; and it is a denial of the testimony to say, 'I will pray myself out of this unfitness into fitness; I will work myself into a right state of mind and character for drawing near to God.'

Were you from this moment to cease from sin, and do nothing but good all the rest of your life, it would be of no avail. Were you to begin praying now, and do nothing else but pray all your days, it would not do. Your own character cannot be your way of approach, nor your ground of confidence toward God. No amount of praying, working, or feeling can satisfy the righteous Law, or pacify a guilty conscience, or quench the flaming sword that guards the access into the presence of the infinitely Holy One.

That which makes it safe for you to draw near to God, and right for God to receive you, must be something altogether away from and *independent of yourself*; for yourself, and everything pertaining to yourself, God has already condemned; and no condemned thing can give you any warrant for going to Him or hoping for acceptance. Your liberty of entrance must come from something that He has accepted, not from something that He has condemned.

I knew an awakened soul who, in the bitterness of his spirit, thus set himself to work and pray in order to get peace. He doubled the amount of his devotions, saying to himself, 'Surely God will give me peace.' But the peace did not come. He set up family worship, saying, 'Surely God will give me peace.' Again the peace did not come. At last he thought of having a prayer-meeting in his house as a certain remedy; he fixed the night, called his neighbours, and prepared himself for conducting the meeting by writing a prayer and learning it by heart. As he finished the operation of learning it, preparatory to the meeting, he threw it down on the table saying, 'Surely *that* will do; God will give me peace now.' In that moment a still small voice seemed to speak in his ear, saying, 'No, that will *not* do; but Christ will do.' Straightaway the scales fell from his eyes and the burden from his shoulders. Peace poured in like a river. 'Christ will do' was his watchword ever after!

Very clear is God's testimony against man, and man's doings, in this great matter of approach and acceptance. 'Not by works of righteousness which we have done,' says Paul in one place (Titus 3:5); 'to him that worketh not,' says he in a second (Rom. 4:5); 'not justified by the works of the law,' says he in a third (Gal. 2:16).

The sinner's peace with God is not to come from his own character. No grounds of peace or elements of reconciliation can be extracted from himself, either directly or indirectly. His one qualification for peace is that he needs it. It is not what he *has* of good, but what he *lacks* of good, that draws him to God; it is the consciousness of this lack that bids him look elsewhere for something both to invite and embolden him to approach. It is our sickness, not our health, that fits us for the physician and casts us upon his skill.

No guilty conscience can be pacified with anything short of that which will make pardon a present, sure, and righteous thing. Can our best doings, our best feelings, our best prayers, our best sacrifices, bring this about? No! Having accumulated these to the utmost, the sinner feels that pardon is just as far off and uncertain as before; and that all his earnestness cannot persuade God to admit him to favour, or bribe his own conscience into true quiet even for an hour.

In all false religion, the worshipper rests his hope of divine favour upon something in his own character, life, or religious duties. The Pharisee did this when he came into the Temple, thanking God that he was 'not as other men'

(Luke 18:11). So do those in our day who expect to get peace by doing, feeling, and praying more than others, or than they themselves have done in time past—and who refuse to take the peace of the free gospel till they have amassed such an amount of doing and feeling as will ease their consciences, and make them conclude that it would not be fair in God to reject the application of men so earnest and devoted as they.

The Galatians did this also when they insisted on adding the Law of Moses to the gospel of Christ, as the ground of confidence toward God. Thus do many act among ourselves. They will not take confidence from God's character or Christ's work, but [will do so] from their own character and work—though in reference to all this it is written, 'The Lord hath rejected thy confidences, and thou shalt not prosper in them' (Jer. 2:37). They object to a present confidence, for that assumes that a sinner's resting-place is wholly outside himself—ready-made, as it were, by God. They would have this confidence to be a very gradual thing, in order that they may gain time and, by a little diligence in religious observances, so add to their stock of duties, prayers, experiences, and devotions that they may, with some 'humble hope' as they call it, claim acceptance from God. By this course of devout living they think they have made themselves more acceptable to God than they were before they began this religious process, and much more entitled to expect the divine favour than those who have not so qualified themselves.

In all this, the attempted resting-place is self, that self which God has condemned. They would not rest upon un-praying, or un-working, or un-devout self; but they think it right and safe to rest upon praying, working, and devout self—and they call this humility! The happy confidence of the simple believer who takes God's Word at once and rests on it, they call presumption or fanaticism; their own miserable uncertainty, extracted from the doings of self, they speak of as a humble hope!

The sinner's own character, in any form and under any process of improvement, cannot furnish reasons for trusting God. However amended, it cannot speak peace to his conscience, nor afford him any warrant for reckoning on God's favour. Nor can it help to heal the breach between him and God, for God can accept nothing but perfection in such a case, and the sinner has nothing but imperfection to present. Imperfect duties and devotions cannot persuade God to forgive.

Besides, be it remembered that the person of the worshipper must be accepted before his services can be acceptable; so that nothing can be of any use to the sinner, save that which provides for personal acceptance completely and at the outset. The sinner must go to God as he is, or not at all. To try to pray himself into something better than a condemned sinner in order to win God's favour, is to make prayer an instrument of self- righteousness; so that, instead of it being the act of an accepted man, it is the price of acceptance, the money that we pay to God for favouring us, and the bribe with which we persuade conscience no longer to trouble us with its terrors.

No knowledge of self, nor consciousness of improvement of self, can soothe the alarms of an awakened conscience or be any ground for expecting the friendship of God. To take comfort from our good doings, good feelings, good intentions, good prayers, or good experiences is to delude ourselves, and to say 'peace' when there is no peace (Jer. 6:14). No man can find rest from his own character, however good; or from his own acts, however religious. Even were he perfect, what enjoyment could there be in thinking about his own perfection? What profit, then, or what peace can there be in thinking about his own *im*-perfection?

Even were there many good things about him, they could not speak peace; for the good things that might speak peace could not make up for the evil things that speak trouble—and what a poor, self-made peace would that be which arose from his thinking as much good and as little evil of himself as possible! And what a temptation, besides, would this furnish to extenuate the evil and exaggerate the good about ourselves; in other words, to deceive our own hearts. Self-deception must always, more or less, be the result of such estimates of our own experiences. Laid open, as we are in such a case, to all manner of self-blinding influences, it is impossible that we can be impartial judges, as in the case of those who are freely and at once forgiven.

One man might say, 'My sins are not very great or many; surely I may have peace.' Another might say, 'I have made up for my sins by my good deeds; I may have peace.' Another might say, 'I have a very deep sense of sin; I may have peace.' Another might say, 'I have repented of my sin; I may have peace.' Another might say, 'I pray much; I work much; I love much; I give much—I may have peace.' What temptation in all this to take the most favourable view of self and its doings! But, after all, it would be vain. There could be no real peace, for the foundation would be sand, not rock. The peace and confidence that come from summing up the good points of our character, or thinking of our good feelings and doings, or setting a certain valuation upon our faith, love, and repentance, must be made up of pride. Its basis is self-righteousness, or at least self-approbation.

It does not mend the matter to say that we look at these good feelings in us as the Spirit's work, not our own. In one aspect this takes away boasting, but in another it does not: It still makes our peace to turn upon what is in ourselves, and not on what is in God. In fact, it makes use of the Holy Spirit for purposes of self-righteousness. It says that the Spirit works the change in us, in order that He may thereby furnish us with a ground of peace within ourselves.

No doubt the Spirit's work in us must be accompanied with peace, but not because He has given us something in ourselves from which to draw our peace. It is that kind of peace which arises unconsciously from the restoration of spiritual health, but not that which Scripture calls 'peace with God' (Rom. 5:1).

It does not arise from *thinking* about the change wrought in us, but unconsciously and involuntarily from the change itself. If a broken limb be made whole, we get relief straight away; not by thinking about the healed member, but simply in the bodily ease and comfort that the cure has given.

So there is a peace arising out of the *change of nature* and character wrought by the Spirit, but this is not reconciliation with God. This is not the peace that the knowledge of forgiveness brings. It accompanies it and flows from it, but the two kinds of peace are quite distinct from each other. Nor does even the peace that attends the restoration of spiritual health come at second-hand from thinking about our change; but directly from the change itself. That change is the soul's new health, and this health is in itself a continual gladness.

Still it remains true, that in ourselves we have no resting place. It is the quality of the work *without*, not the quality of that *within*, which satisfies us. 'No confidence in the flesh' must be our motto, as it is the foundation of God's gospel (Phil. 3:3).

3

God's Character Our Resting Place

We have seen that a sinner's peace cannot come from himself, from the knowledge of himself, from thinking about his own acts and feelings, from believing in his own faith, nor from the consciousness of any amendment of his old self.

Whence, then, is it to come? How does he get it?

It can only come from God, and it is in *knowing God* that he gets it. God has written a Volume for the purpose of making Himself known, and it is in this revelation of His character that the sinner is to find the rest that he is seeking. God Himself is the fountain-head of our peace; His revealed truth is the channel through which this peace finds its way to us; and His Holy Spirit is the great Interpreter of that truth to us. 'Acquaint now thyself with him [i.e., God], and be at peace' (Job 22:21). Yes, acquaintance with God is peace!

Had God told us that He was not gracious, that He took no interest in our welfare, and that He had no intention of pardoning us, we could have had no peace and no hope. In that case our knowing God would only make us miserable. Our situation would be like that of the devils, who 'believe, and tremble' (James 2:19)—and the more that we knew of such a God, we should tremble the more; for how fearful a thing must it be to have the great God that made us, the great Father of spirits, against us, not for us!

Strange to say, this is the very state of disquietude in which we find many who yet profess to believe in a God 'merciful and gracious' (Exod. 34:6)! With the Bible in their hands, and the cross before their eyes, they wander on in a state of darkness and fear, just such as would have arisen had God revealed Himself in hatred, not in love. They seem to believe the very opposite of what the Bible teaches us concerning God, and to attach a meaning to the cross the reverse of what the gospel affirms it really bears. Had God been all frowns, the Bible all terrors, and Christ all sternness, these men could not have been in a more troubled and uncertain state than that in which they are.

How is this? Have they not misunderstood the Bible? Have they not mistaken the character of God, looking on Him as an 'austere man' and a 'hard master'? Are they not labouring to supplement the grace of God by something on their part, as if they believed that this grace was not sufficient to meet their case, until they had attracted it to themselves by some earnest performances, gloomy experiences, alarming convictions, or spiritual exercises of their own?

God has declared Himself to be gracious. 'God is love' (1 John 4:16). He has embodied this grace in the person and work of His beloved Son. He has told us that this grace is for the ungodly, the unholy, the rebellious, the dead in sin. The more, then, that we know of this God and of His grace, the more will His peace fill us. Nor will the greatness of our sins and the hardness of our hearts, or the changeableness of our feelings, discourage or disquiet, however much they may humble us and make us dissatisfied with ourselves.

Let us study the character of God. He is:

- holy, yet loving—the love not interfering with the holiness, nor the holiness with the love;
- absolutely sovereign, yet infinitely gracious—the sovereignty not limiting the grace, nor grace relaxing the sovereignty;
- drawing the unwilling, yet not hindering the willing, if any such there be;
- quickening whom He will, yet having no pleasure in the death of the wicked;
- compelling some to come in, yet freely inviting all!

Let us look at Him in the face of Jesus Christ, for He is the express image of His person, and he that has seen Him has seen the Father. The knowledge of that gracious character, as interpreted by the cross of Christ, is the true remedy for our disquietudes. Insufficient acquaintanceship with God lies at the root of our fears and gloom.

I know that flesh and blood cannot reveal God to you, and that the Holy Spirit alone can enable you, to know either the Father or the Son. But I would not have you for a moment suppose that the Spirit is reluctant to do His work in you. Nor would I encourage you in the awful thought that you are willing, while He is unwilling; or that the sovereignty of God is a hindrance to the sinner and a restraint of the Spirit. The whole Bible takes for granted that all this is absolutely impossible. Never can the great truths of divine sovereignty and the Spirit's work land us, as some seem to think they may do, in such a conflict between a willing sinner and an unwilling God.

The whole Bible is so written by the Spirit, and the gospel was so preached by the apostles, as never to raise the question of God's willingness, nor to lead to the remotest suspicion of His readiness to furnish the sinner with all needed aid. Hence the great truths of God's eternal election and Christ's redemption of His Church, as we read them in the Bible, are helps and encouragements to the soul. But, interpreted as they are by many, they seem barrier-walls, not ladders for scaling the great barrier-walls of man's unwillingness; and anxious souls become land-locked in metaphysical questions and self-righteous perplexities, out of which there can be no way of extrication, save that of taking God at His word.

In the Bible, God has revealed Himself. In Christ, He has done so most expressively. He has done so, that there might be no mistake as to His character on the part of man.

Christ's person is a revelation of God. Christ's work is a revelation of God. Christ's words are a revelation of God. He is in the Father and the Father in Him. His words and works are the words and works of the Father. In the manger He showed us God. In the synagogue of Nazareth He showed us God. At Jacob's well He showed us God. At the tomb of Lazarus He showed us God. On Olivet, as He wept over Jerusalem, He showed us God. On the cross He showed us God. In the tomb He showed us God. In His resurrection He showed us God. If we say with Philip, 'Show us the Father, and it sufficeth us'; He answers, 'Have I been so long time with you, and yet hast thou not known me? He that hath seen me hath seen the Father' (John 14:8-9). This God whom Christ reveals as the God of righteous grace and gracious righteousness, is the God with whom we have to do (Heb. 4:13).

To know His character, as thus interpreted to us by Jesus and His cross, is to have peace. It is into this knowledge of the Father that the Holy Spirit leads the soul whom He is conducting, by His almighty power, from darkness to light—for everything that we know of God we owe to this divine Teacher, this Interpreter. But never let the sinner imagine that he is more willing to learn than the Spirit is to teach. Never let him say to himself, 'I would know God, but I cannot of myself, and the Spirit will not teach me.'

It is not enough for us to say to a dispirited person, 'It is your unbelief that is keeping you wretched; only believe, and all is well.' This is true, but it is only *general* truth, which in many cases is of no use because it does not show him how it applies to him. On this point, he is often at fault, thinking that faith is some great work to be done, which he is to labour at with all his might, praying all the while to God to help him in doing this great work—and that unbelief is some evil principle requiring to be uprooted before the gospel will be of any use to him.

But what is the real meaning of this faith and this unbelief ?

In all unbelief there are these two things: a good opinion of one's self and a bad opinion of God. So long as these two things exist, it is impossible for an inquirer to find rest. His good opinion of himself makes him think it quite possible to win God's favour by his own religious performances; and his bad opinion of God makes him unwilling and afraid to put his case wholly into His hands. The object of the Holy Spirit's work, in convincing of sin, is to alter the sinner's opinion of himself, and so to reduce his estimate of his own character that he shall think of himself as God does—and so cease to suppose it possible that he can be justified by any excellency of his own. Having altered the sinner's good opinion of himself, the Spirit then alters his evil opinion of God, so as to make him see that the God with whom he has to do is really the God of all grace (1 Pet. 5:10).

But the inquirer denies that he has a good opinion of himself, and [instead he says that he] owns himself a sinner. Now, a man may *say* this, but really to *know* it is something more than saying. Besides, he may be willing to take the name of sinner to himself, in common with his fellowmen, and yet not at all own himself such a sinner as God says he is: such a sinner as needs a whole Saviour to himself; such a sinner as needs the cross, blood, and righteousness of the Son of God. He may not have quite such a bad opinion of himself as to make him aware that he can expect nothing from God on the score of personal goodness, amendment of life, devout observance of duty, or superiority to others. It takes a great deal to destroy a man's good opinion of himself; and even after he has lost his good opinion of his works, he retains his good opinion of his heart. And even after he has lost that, he holds fast his good opinion of his religious duties, by means of which he hopes to make up for evil works and a bad heart. He hopes to be able so to act, feel, and pray as to lead God to entertain a good opinion of him and receive him into favour.

All such efforts spring from thinking well of himself in some measure; and also from his thinking evil of God, as if He would not receive him as he is. If he knew himself as God does, he would no more resort to such efforts than he would think of walking up an Alpine precipice. How difficult it is to make a man think of himself as God does! What but the almightiness of the divine Spirit can accomplish this?

But the inquirer says that he has not a bad opinion of God. Has he, however, such an opinion of Him as the Bible gives, or the cross reveals? Has he such an opinion of Him as makes him feel quite safe in putting his soul into His gracious hands, and trusting Him with its eternal keeping? If not, where is his good opinion of God? Surely the knowledge of God that the cross supplies ought to set all doubt aside, and make distrust appear in the most odious of aspects: as a wretched misrepresentation of God's character and a slander upon His gracious name.

Unbelief is thus the belief of a lie and the rejection of the truth. It obliterates from the cross the gracious name of God, and inscribes another name, that of an unknown god in which there is no peace for the sinner, no rest for the weary.

Accept, then, the character of God as given in the gospel. Read aright His blessed name as it is written upon the cross. Take the simple interpretation given of His mind toward the ungodly as you have it, at length, in the glad tidings of peace. Is not that enough? If that which God has made known of Himself be not enough to allay your fears, nothing else will. The Holy Spirit will not give you peace irrespective of your views of God's character. That would be countenancing the worship of a false god, instead of the true God revealed in the Bible. It is in connection with the truth concerning the true God, 'the God of all grace' (1 Pet. 5:10), that the Spirit gives peace. It is the love of the *true God* that He sheds abroad in the heart.

The object of the Spirit's work is to make us acquainted with the true Jehovah, that in Him we may rest—not to produce in us certain feelings, the consciousness of which will make us think better of ourselves and give us confidence toward God. That which He shows us of ourselves is only evil; that which He shows us of God is only good. He does not enable us to feel or to believe in order that we may be comforted by our feeling or our faith. Even when working in us most powerfully, He turns our eye away from His own work in us, to fix it on God and His love in Christ Jesus our Lord. The substance of the gospel is the name of the great Jehovah, unfolded in and by Jesus Christ, the *character* of Him in whom we 'live and move and have our being' (Acts 17:28), as the 'just God' and the 'Saviour' (Isa. 45:21), the Justifier of the ungodly (Rom. 5:6).

Inquiring spirit, turn your eye to the cross and see these two things: the crucifiers and the Crucified. See the crucifiers, the haters of God and of His Son: they are *yourself.* Read in them your own character, and cease to think of making that a ground of peace. See the Crucified: it is God Himself, incarnate love. It is He who made you, God manifest in flesh, suffering, dying for the ungodly (Rom 5:6). Can you suspect His grace? Can you cherish evil thoughts of Him? Can you ask anything further to awaken in you the fullest and most unreserved confidence? Will you misinterpret that agony and death by saying either that they do not mean grace, or that the grace which they mean is not for you? Call to mind that which is written: 'Hereby perceive we the love of God, because he laid down his life for us' (1 John 3:16). 'Herein is love, not that we loved God, but that he loved us, and sent his Son to be the propitiation for our sins' (1 John 4:10).

41

4

Righteous Grace

We have spoken of God's character as 'the God of all grace' (1 Pet. 5:10). We have seen that it is in 'tasting that the Lord is gracious' that the sinner has peace (1 Pet. 2:3).

But let us keep in mind that this grace is the grace of a *righteous* God; it is the grace of one who is Judge as well as Father. Unless we see this, we shall mistake the gospel, and fail in appreciating both the pardon we are seeking and the great sacrifice through which it comes to us. No vague forgiveness, arising out of mere paternal love or good-natured indifference to sin, will do. We need to know what kind of pardon it is, and whether it proceeds from the full recognition of our absolute guiltiness by Him who is to 'judge the world in righteousness' (Acts 17:31). The right kind of pardon comes not from love alone, but from law; not from good-nature, but from righteousness; not from indifference to sin, but from holiness.

The inquirer who is only half in earnest overlooks this. His feelings are moved, but his conscience is not roused. Hence he is content with very vague ideas of God's mere compassion for the sinner's unhappiness. To him human guilt seems but human misfortune, and God's acquittal of the sinner little more than the overlooking of his sin. He does not trouble himself with asking how the forgiveness comes, or what is the real nature of the love that he professes to have received. He is easily soothed to sleep because he has never been fully awake. He is, at the best, a stony-ground hearer, soon losing the poor measure of joy that he may have gotten (Mark 4:16-17)—becoming a formalist, or perhaps a trifler with sin, or, it may be, a religious sentimentalist.

But he whose conscience has been pierced is not so easily satisfied. He sees that the God whose favour he is seeking is holy as well as loving, and that He has to do with righteousness as well as grace. Hence the first inquiry he makes is as to the righteousness of the pardon that the grace of God holds out. He must be satisfied on this point and see that the grace is righteous grace, before he can enjoy it at all. The more alive that he is to his own unrighteousness, the more does he feel the need of ascertaining the righteousness of the grace that we make known to him.

It does not satisfy him to say that, since it comes from a righteous God, it must be righteous grace. His conscience wants to see the righteousness of the way by which it comes. Without this it cannot be pacified or 'purged'; and the man is not made 'perfect as pertaining to the conscience' (Heb. 9:9-14), but must always have an uneasy feeling that all is not right—that his sins may one day rise up against him.

That which soothes the heart will not always pacify the conscience. The sight of the grace will do the former, but only the sight of the righteousness of the grace will do the latter. Till the latter is done, there cannot be real peace.

Here the work of Christ comes in; and the cross of the Sin-bearer answers the question that conscience had raised: 'Is it *righteous* grace?' It is this great work of propitiation that exhibits God as 'the just God, and the Saviour' (Isa. 45:21), not only righteous in spite of His justifying the ungodly, but righteous *in* doing so. It shows salvation as an act of righteousness; indeed, one of the highest acts of righteousness that a righteous God can do. It shows pardon not only as the deed of a righteous God, but as *the* thing that declares how righteous He is, and how He hates and condemns the very sin that He is pardoning.

Hear the Word of the Lord concerning this 'finished' work.

- 'Christ died for our sins' (1 Cor. 15:3).
- 'He was wounded for our transgressions, he was bruised for our iniquities' (Isa. 53:5).
- 'Christ was once offered to bear the sins of many' (Heb. 9:28).
- 'He gave himself for us' (Titus 2:14).
- He 'was delivered for our offences' (Rom. 4:25).
- He 'gave himself for our sins' (Gal. 1:4).
- 'Christ died for the ungodly' (Rom. 5:6).

- 'He appeared to put away sin by the sacrifice of himself' (Heb. 9:26).
- 'Christ hath suffered for us in the flesh' (1 Pet. 4:1).
- 'Christ also hath once suffered for sins, the just for the unjust' (1 Pet. 3:18).
- 'His own self bare our sins in his own body on the tree' (1 Pet. 2:24).

These expressions speak of something more than love. Love is in each of them, the deep, true, real love of God; but also justice and holiness, the inflexible and inexorable adherence to Law. They have no meaning apart from *law*: law as the foundation, pillar, and keystone of the universe.

But their connection with law is also their connection with love. For, as it was Law, in its unchangeable perfection, that created the necessity for the Surety's death, so it was this necessity that drew out the Surety's love, and gave also glorious proof of the love of Him who made Him to be sin for us (2 Cor. 5:21). For if a man were to die for another when there was no necessity for his doing so, we should hardly call his death a proof of love. At best, such would be foolish love, or at least a fond and idle way of showing it. But to die for one when there is really need of dying, is the true test of genuine love. To die for a friend when nothing less will save him, this is the proof of love! When either he or we *must* die, and when he, to save us from dying, dies himself—this is love. There was need of a death if we were to be saved from dying; righteousness made the necessity. And, to meet this terrible necessity, the Son of God took flesh and died! He died because it was written, 'The soul that sinneth, it shall die' (Ezek. 18:4). Love led Him down to the cradle; love led Him up to the cross! He died as the sinner's Substitute. He died to make it a righteous thing in God to cancel the sinner's guilt, and annul the penalty of his everlasting death.

Had it not been for this dying, grace and guilt could not have looked each other in the face; God and the sinner could not have come near; righteousness would have forbidden reconciliation—and righteousness, we know, is as divine and real a thing as love. Without this expiation, it would not have been right for God to receive the sinner, nor safe for the sinner to come.

But now, mercy and truth have met together (Ps. 85:10); now grace is righteousness, and righteousness is grace. This *satisfies the sinner's conscience* by showing him righteous love for the unrighteous and unlovable. It tells him, too, that the reconciliation brought about in this way shall never be disturbed, either in this life or that which is to come. It is righteous reconciliation and will stand every test, as well as last throughout eternity. The peace of conscience, thus secured, will be trial-proof, sickness-proof, deathbed-proof, judgment-proof. Realizing this, the chief of sinners can say, 'Who is he that condemneth?' (Rom. 8:34).

What peace for the stricken conscience is there in the truth that Christ died for the *ungodly*, and that it is of the *ungodly* that the righteous God is the Justifier! The righteous grace, thus coming to us through the sin-bearing work of the Word 'made flesh' (John 1:14), tells the soul, at once and forever, that there can be no condemnation for any sinner upon earth who will only consent to be indebted to this free love of God, which, like a fountain of living water, is bursting out freely from the foot of the cross.

Just, yet the Justifier of the ungodly (Rom. 4:5)! What glad tidings are here! Here is grace, God's free love to the sinner, divine bounty and goodwill—altogether irrespective of human worth or merit. For this is the scriptural meaning of that often misunderstood word *grace*.

This righteous free-love has its origin in the bosom of the Father, where the only-begotten Son has His dwelling (John 1:18). It is not produced by anything outside of God Himself. It was man's evil, not his good, that called it forth. It is not the like drawing to the like, but to the unlike; it is light attracted by darkness, and life by death. It does not wait for our seeking, it comes *unasked* as well as *undeserved.* It is not our faith that creates it or calls it up; our faith realizes it as already existing in its divine and manifold fulness. Whether we believe it or not, this righteous grace exists, and exists for us. Unbelief refuses it; but faith takes it, rejoices in it, and lives upon it.

Yes, faith takes this righteous grace of God, and with it a righteous pardon, a righteous salvation, and a righteous heirship of the everlasting glory.

5

THE BLOOD OF SPRINKLING

An inquirer asks, 'What is the special meaning of the *blood*, of which we read so much? How does it speak of peace? How does it "purge your conscience from dead works" (Heb. 9:14)? What can blood have to do with the peace, the grace, and the righteousness of which we have been speaking?'

God has given the reason for the stress that He lays upon the blood; and, in understanding this, we get to the very bottom of the grounds of a sinner's peace.

The sacrifices of old, from the days of Abel onwards, furnish us with the key to the meaning of the blood, and explain the necessity for its being 'shed for the remission of sins'. 'Not without blood' (Heb. 9:7) was the great truth taught by God from the beginning, the inscription which may be said to have been written on the gates of the Tabernacle and the Temple. For more than two thousand years, during the ages of the patriarchs, there was but one great sacrifice—the burnt-offering. This, under the Mosaic service, was split into parts—the peace-offering, trespass-offering, and sin-offering. In all of these, however, the essence of the original burnt-offering was preserved—by the blood and the fire that were common to them all. The blood, as the emblem of substitution, and the fire, as the symbol of God's wrath upon the substitute, were seen in all the parts of Israel's service; but especially in the daily burnt-offering—the morning and evening lamb—which was the true continuation and representative of the old patriarchal burnt-offering. It was to this that John referred when he said, 'Behold the Lamb of God, which taketh away the sin of the world' (John 1:29). Israel's daily lamb was the kernel and core of all the Old Testament sacrifices, and it was its blood that carried the worshippers back to the primitive sacrifices, and forward to the blood of sprinkling that was to speak better things than that of Abel (Heb. 12:24).

In all these sacrifices the shedding of the blood was the infliction of *death*. The 'blood was the life' (Lev. 17:11, 14; Deut. 12:23), and the pouring out of the blood was 'the pouring out of the soul' (Isa. 53:12). This blood-shedding, or life-taking, was the payment of the penalty for sin; for it was threatened from the beginning, 'In the day that thou eatest thereof thou shalt surely die' (Gen. 2:17); and it is written, 'The soul that sinneth, it shall die' (Ezek. 18:4); and again, 'The wages of sin is death' (Rom. 6:23).

But the blood-shedding of Israel's sacrifices could not take sin away. It showed the way in which this was to be done, but it was in fact more a 'remembrance of sins' (Heb. 10:3), than an expiation (Heb. 10:11). It said life must be given for life before sin can be pardoned; but then the continual repetition of the sacrifices showed that there was needed 'richer blood' than the Temple altar was ever sprinkled with, and a more precious life than man could give.

The great blood-shedding has been accomplished; the better life has been presented; and the *one* death of the Son of God has done what all the deaths of old could never do. His one life was enough, His one dying paid the penalty—and God does not ask two lives, or two deaths, or two payments. 'Christ was once offered to bear the sins of many' (Heb. 9:28). 'In that he died, he died unto sin once' (Rom. 6:10). He 'offered one sacrifice for sins for ever' (Heb. 10:12).

The 'sprinkling of the blood' (Exod. 24:8) was the making use of the death by putting it upon certain persons or things, so that these persons or things were counted to be dead, and therefore to have paid the Law's penalty. So long as they had not paid that penalty, they were counted unclean and unfit for God to look upon; but as soon as they had paid it, they were counted clean and fit for the service of God. Usually when we read of cleansing, we think merely of our common process of removing dirt by water and soap. But this is not the figure meant in the application of the sacrifice. The blood cleanses by making us partakers of the death of the Substitute. For what is it that makes us filthy before God? It is our guilt, our breach of law, and our being under sentence of death in consequence of our disobedience. We have not only done what God dislikes, but what His righteous Law declares to be worthy of death. It is this sentence of death that separates us so completely from God—making it wrong for Him to bless us, and perilous for us to go to Him.

When thus covered all over with that guilt whose penalty is death, the blood is brought in by the great High Priest. That blood represents death; it is God's expression for death. It is then sprinkled on us, and thus death, which is the Law's penalty, passes on us. We die. We undergo the sentence, and thus the guilt passes away. We are cleansed! The sin which was like scarlet becomes as snow, and that which was like crimson becomes as wool (Isa. 1:18). It is thus that we make use of the blood of Christ in believing, for faith is just the sinner employing the blood. Believing what God has testified concerning this blood, we become one with Jesus in His death; and thus we are counted in law, and treated by God, as men who have paid the whole penalty, and so been washed from their sins in his blood (Rev. 1:5).[1]

Such are the glad tidings of life, through Him who died. They are tidings that tell us, not what we are to *do*, in order

---

1   It is interesting to notice, in connection with this point, that the old Scotch terms in law for acquitting and condemning were 'cleanse' and 'fyle' (that is, defile). In the assize held upon the faithful ministers of the Church of Scotland in 1606, it was put to the court whether these said ministers should be 'clenzed' or 'fyled,' and the chancellor 'declared that they were fyled by manliest votes.' See Calderwood, vol. vi., 388.

to be saved, but what He *has done.* This only can lay to rest the sinner's fears, can purge his conscience (Heb. 9:14), can make him feel as a thoroughly pardoned man. The right knowledge of God's meaning in this sprinkling of the blood is the only effective way of removing the anxieties of the troubled soul, and of introducing it into perfect peace.

The gospel is not the mere revelation of the heart of God in Christ Jesus. In it the righteousness of God is specially manifested (Rom. 1:17), and it is this revelation of the righteousness that makes it so truly 'the power of God unto salvation' (Rom. 1:16). The blood-shedding is God's declaration of the righteousness of the love that He is pouring down upon the sons of men; it is the reconciliation of law and love; the condemnation of the sin and the acquittal of the sinner. As 'without shedding of blood there is no remission' (Heb. 9:22), so the gospel announces that the blood has been shed by which remission flows to us; and now we know that 'the blood of Christ his son cleanses us from all sin' (1 John 1:7). The conscience is satisfied. It feels that God's grace is righteous grace, that His love is holy love. There it rests.

It is not by incarnation, but by blood-shedding that we are saved. The Christ of God is no mere expounder of wisdom, no mere deliverer or gracious benefactor; and they who think that they have told the whole gospel when they have spoken of Jesus revealing the love of God, greatly err.

If Christ is not the Substitute, He is nothing to the sinner. If He did not die as the Sin-bearer, He has died in vain. Let us not be deceived on this point, nor misled by those who, when they announce Christ as the Deliverer, think they have preached the gospel. If I throw a rope to a drowning man, I am a deliverer. But is Christ no more than that? If I cast myself into the sea, and risk myself to save another, I am a deliverer. But is Christ no more? Did He but *risk* His life? The very essence of Christ's deliverance is the substitution of Himself for us, His life for ours. He did not come to *risk* His life; He came to die! He did not redeem us by a little loss, a little sacrifice, a little labour, a little suffering: 'He redeemed us to God by his blood,' 'the precious blood of Christ' (1 Pet. 1:19). He gave all He had, even His life, for us. This is the kind of deliverance that awakens the happy song, 'Unto him that loved us, and washed us from our sins in his own blood' (Rev. 1:5; 5:9).

The tendency of the world's religion just now is to reject the blood, and to glory in a gospel that needs no sacrifice, no 'Lamb slain' (Rev. 13:8). Thus, they go the way of Cain, who refused the blood, and came to God without it. He would not own himself a sinner condemned to die and needing the death of another to save him. This was man's open rejection of God's way [to] life. Foremost in this rejection we see the first murderer—and he who would not defile his altar with the blood of a lamb, pollutes the earth with his brother's blood.

The heathen altars have been red with blood; and to this day they are the same. But these worshippers do not know what they mean in bringing that blood. It is associated only with *vengeance* in their minds; and they shed it to appease the vengeance of their gods. But this is no recognition either of the love or the righteousness of God. 'Fury is not in' Him (Isa. 27:4), whereas their altars speak only of fury. The blood which they bring is a denial both of righteousness and grace.

But look at Israel's altars. There is blood; and they who bring it know the God to whom they come. They bring it in acknowledgment of their own guilt, but also of His pardoning love. They say, 'I deserve death; but let this death stand for mine; and let the love that otherwise could not reach me, by reason of guilt, now pour itself out on me.'

Inquiring soul! Beware of Cain's error on the one hand, in coming to God without blood; and beware of the heathen error on the other, in mistaking the meaning of the blood. Understand God's mind and meaning in 'the precious blood' of His Son. Believe His testimony concerning it; so shall your conscience be pacified and your soul find rest.

It is into Christ's *death* that we are baptized (Rom. 6:3), and hence the cross, which was the instrument of that death, is that in which we glory. The cross is to us the payment of the sinner's penalty, the extinction of the debt, and the tearing up of the handwriting which was against us. And as the cross is the payment, so the resurrection is God's receipt in full, for the whole sum, signed with His own hand. Our faith is not the completion of the payment, but the simple recognition on our part of the payment made by the Son of God. By this recognition we become as one with Him who died and rose, that we are thereafter reckoned to be the parties who have paid the penalty, and treated as if it were we ourselves who had died. Thus are we 'justified from sin', and then made partakers of the righteousness of Him, who was not only delivered for our offences, but who was raised again for our justification.

6

THE PERSON AND WORK OF THE SUBSTITUTE

Life comes to us through death, and thus grace abounds towards us in righteousness. This we have seen in a general way. But we have something more to learn concerning Him who lived and died as the sinner's Substitute. The more that we know of His person and His work, the more shall we be satisfied, in heart and conscience, with the provision that God has made for our great need.

Our Sin-bearer is the eternal Son of God. Of Him it is written, 'In the beginning was the Word, and the Word was with God, and the Word was God' (John 1:1). He is 'the brightness of his glory, and the express image of his person' (Heb. 1:3). He is 'in the Father, and the Father in him'; 'the Father dwelleth in him'; 'he that hath seen him hath seen the Father' (John 14:9-11); and 'he that heareth him, heareth him that sent him' (Luke 10:16). He is 'the Word...made flesh' (John 1:14); 'God...manifest in the flesh' (1 Tim. 3:16); 'Jesus Christ...come in the flesh'

(1 John 4:2-3). His name is 'Immanuel', God with us (Isa. 7:14; Matt. 1:23); Jesus, the Saviour (Matt. 1:21); 'Christ', the anointed One, filled with the Spirit without measure (John 3:34); 'the only-begotten of the Father, full of grace and truth' (John 1:14).

He came preaching 'the gospel of the kingdom', that is, the good news about the kingdom (Mark 1:14); teaching the multitudes that gathered round Him (Mark 4:1); healing the sick, opening the eyes of the blind, and raising the dead (Matt. 4:23,24); receiving sinners, and eating with them (Luke 15:2). He came 'to seek and save that which was lost' (Luke 19:10); He went about speaking words of grace such as never man spake, saying, 'I am the way, the truth, and the life: no man cometh unto the Father, but by me' (John 14:6).

He went out and in as the Saviour; and in His whole life we see Him as the shepherd seeking His lost sheep, as the woman searching for her lost piece of silver, and as the father looking out for his lost son. He is 'mighty to save' (Isa. 63:1); He is 'able also to save them to the uttermost' (Heb. 7:25); He came to be 'the Saviour of the world' (1 John 4:14).

In all these things, thus written concerning Jesus, there is good news for the sinner such as should draw him, in simple confidence, to God; making him feel that his case has really been taken up in earnest by God; and that God's thoughts toward him are thoughts, not of anger, but of peace and grace. Heaven has come down to earth! There is goodwill toward man. He is not to be handed over to his great enemy. God has taken his side, and stepped in between him and Satan. This world is not to be destroyed, nor all its dwellers made eternal exiles from God! The darkness is passing away, and the true light is shining!

Yet it is not the person of Christ, nor His birth, nor His life, that can suffice. That the Son of God took a true but sinless humanity, of the very substance of the virgin; becoming bone of our bone and flesh of our flesh (Gen. 2:23); being in very deed the woman's seed; that He dwelt among us for a lifetime—is but the beginning of the good news, the Alpha but not the Omega. This was shown to Israel, and to us also, in the Temple veil. That veil was the type of His flesh (Heb. 10:20); and so long as that curtain remained whole, there was no entrance into the place of the near presence of God. The worshipper was not indeed frowned upon, but he had to stand at a distance. The veil said to the sinner, Godhead is within; but it also said, You cannot enter till something more has been done. The Holy Ghost, by it, signified that the way into the holiest was not yet open. The rending of the veil, that is, the crucifixion of 'the Word made flesh', opened the way completely.

Hence it is that the Holy Spirit sums up the good news in one or two special points. They are these: Christ was crucified; Christ died; Christ was buried; Christ arose again from the dead; Christ went up on high; Christ sits at God's right hand—our 'advocate with the Father' (1 John 2:1), 'ever living to make intercession' for us (Heb. 7:25; cf. Rom. 8:34).

These are the great facts that contain the good news. They are few and they are plain, so that a child may remember and understand them. They are the caskets that contain the heavenly gems. They are the cups that hold the living water for the thirsty soul, the golden basket in which God has placed the bread of life, the true 'bread which came down from heaven', of which if a man eat he shall never die (John 6:58). They are the volumes in whose brief but precious pages are written the records of God's mighty mercy; records so simple that even a 'fool' may read and comprehend them; so true and sure that all the wisdom of the world, and all the wiles of hell, cannot shake their certainty.

The knowledge of these is salvation. On them we rest our confidence, for they are the revelation of the *name* of God; and it is written, 'They that know thy name will put their trust in thee' (Ps. 9:10).

Let us listen to apostolic preaching, and see how these facts form the heads of the first sermons, sermons such as Peter's at Jerusalem, or Paul's at Corinth and Antioch. Peter's sermon at Jerusalem (Acts 2:29-36) was that Jesus of Nazareth, who was crucified, had been raised from the dead and exalted to the throne of God, being made both Lord and Christ. This the apostle declared to be 'good news'. Paul's sermon at Antioch was in substance the same: a statement of the facts regarding the death and resurrection of Jesus. The application of that sermon was in these words, 'Be it known unto you therefore, men and brethren, that through this man is preached unto you the forgiveness of sins: and by him all that believe are justified' (Acts 13:38-39). He gives us elsewhere the following sketch of his preaching: 'Moreover, brethren, I declare unto you the gospel which I preached unto you...how that Christ died for our sins according to the scriptures; and that he was buried, and that he rose again the third day according to the scriptures' (1 Cor. 15:1-4). Then he adds: 'So we preach, and so ye believed' (v. 11).

Such was apostolic preaching. Such was Paul's gospel. It narrated a few facts respecting Christ, adding the evidence of their truth and certainty [so] that all who heard might believe and be saved. In these facts, the free love of God to sinners is announced; and the great salvation is revealed. It is this gospel that is 'the power of God unto salvation to every one that believeth...for therein is the righteousness of God revealed from faith to faith' (Rom. 1:16-17).

Its burden was not, 'Do this, or do that; labour and pray, and use the means'—that is law, not gospel. But Christ has done all! He did it all when He 'was delivered for our offences, and was raised again for our justification' (Rom. 4:25). He did it all when He 'made peace through the blood of his cross' (Col. 1:20). 'It is finished' (John 19:30). His doing is so complete that it has left nothing for us to do. We have but to enter into the joy of knowing that all is done! 'This is the record, that God hath given to us eternal life, and this life is in his Son' (1 John 5:11).

But let us gather together some of the true 'sayings of God' concerning Christ and His work. In these we shall find the divine interpretation of the facts above referred to.

We shall see the meaning which the Holy Spirit attaches to these, and so our faith shall not 'stand in the wisdom of men, but in the power of God' (1 Cor. 2:5). It was in this way that the Lord Himself, before He left the earth, removed the unbelief of the doubters around Him. He reminded them of the written Word, 'Thus it is written, and thus it behoved [the] Christ to suffer, and to rise from the dead the third day: and that repentance and remission of sins should be preached in his name among all nations, beginning at Jerusalem' (Luke 24:46-47).

Hear, then, the Word of the Lord! For heaven and earth shall pass away, but these words shall not pass away (Matt. 24:35): 'God hath not appointed us to wrath, but to obtain salvation by our Lord Jesus Christ, who *died for us*, that, whether we wake or sleep, we should live together with him' (1 Thess. 5:9-10). 'By the which will we are sanctified *through the offering of the body of Jesus Christ* once for all' (Heb. 10:10). 'In due time Christ *died* for the ungodly' (Rom. 5:6). 'It is Christ that *died*, yea rather, that is *risen again*, who is even at the right hand of God, who also maketh intercession for us' (Rom. 8:34). 'Who *gave himself* for our sins' (Gal. 1:4). 'Christ hath redeemed us from the curse of the law, being *made a curse* for us' (Gal. 3:13). 'In whom *we have redemption through his blood*, the forgiveness of sins, according to the riches of his grace' (Eph. 1:7).

'He humbled himself, and became *obedient unto death*, even the death of the cross' (Phil. 2:8). 'Remember that Jesus Christ of the seed of David was *raised from the dead* according to my gospel' (2 Tim. 2:8). 'Who *gave himself* for us' (Titus 2:14). 'Christ was *once offered* to bear the sins of many' (Heb. 9:28). 'Jesus also, that he might sanctify the people *with his own blood*, suffered without the gate' (Heb. 13:12). 'Christ also *suffered* for us' (1 Pet. 2:21). 'Who his own self *bare our sins* in his own body on the tree' (1 Pet. 2:24). 'Christ also hath once *suffered for sins*, the just for the unjust' (1 Pet. 3:18). 'Christ hath *suffered for us* in the flesh' (1 Pet. 4:1). 'He is the *propitiation* for our sins' (1 John 2:2). 'Unto him that loved us, and washed us from our sins *in his own blood*' (Rev. 1:5). 'I am he that liveth, and *was dead*; and, behold, *I am alive for evermore*' (Rev. 1:18). 'Thou wast *slain*, and hast redeemed us to God *by thy blood*' (Rev. 5:9).

These are all divine truths, written in divine words. These sayings are faithful and true; they come from Him that cannot lie; and they are as true in these last days as they were when first written, for 'the word of our God shall stand for ever' (Isa. 40:8; cf. 1 Pet. 1:25). In them we find the authentic exposition of the facts that the apostles preached; and, in that, we learn the glad tidings concerning the way in which salvation from a righteous God has come to unrighteous man. Jesus died—that is the paying of the debt, the endurance of the penalty, the death for death. He was buried—that is the proof that His death was a true death, needing a tomb as we do. He rose again—this is God's declaration that He, the righteous Judge, is satisfied with the payment, no less than with Him who made it.

Could there be better, gladder news to the sinner than this? What more can he ask to satisfy him than that which has so fully satisfied the holy Lord God of earth and heaven? If this will not avail, then he can expect no more. If this is not enough, then Christ has died in vain.

God has thus brought 'near his righteousness' (Isa. 46:13). We do not need to go up to heaven for it; that would imply that Christ had never come down. Nor do we need to go down to the depths of the earth for it; that would say that Christ had never been buried and never risen. It is near. It is as near as is the Word concerning it, which enters into our ears (Rom. 10:8). We do not need to exert ourselves to bring it near, nor to do anything to attract it towards us. It is already so near, so very near, that we cannot bring it closer. If we try to get up warm feelings and good dispositions, in order to remove some fancied remainder of distance, we shall fail; not simply because these actings of ours cannot do what we are trying to do, but because there is no need of any such effort. The thing is done already. God has brought His righteousness near to the sinner. The office of faith is not *to work*, but to *cease working*; not to *do* anything, but to *own that all is done*; not to bring near the righteousness, but to rejoice in it as already near. This is 'the word of the truth of the gospel' (Col. 1:5).

7

THE WORD OF THE TRUTH OF THE GOSPEL

How shall I come before God and stand in His presence, with happy confidence on my part, and gracious acceptance on His?

This is the sinner's question, and he asks it because he knows that there is guilt between him and God. No doubt this was Adam's question when he stitched his fig-leaves together for a covering (Gen. 3:7-8). But he was soon made to feel that the fig-leaves would not do. He must be wholly covered, not in part only; and that by something which even God's eye cannot see through. As God comes near, the uselessness of his fig-leaves is felt, and he rushes into the thick foliage to hide from the divine eye. The Lord approaches the trembling man, and makes him feel that this hiding-place will not do. Then He begins to tell him what will do. He announces a better covering and a better hiding-place. He reveals Himself as the God of grace, the God who hates sin, yet who takes the sinner's side against the sinner's enemy, the old serpent. And all this through the seed of the woman, the man who is the true 'hiding-place' (Isa. 32:2). Adam can now leave his thicket safely, and feel that in this revealed grace he can stand before God without fear or shame. He has heard the good news, and brief as it is, it has restored his confidence and removed his alarm.

Let us hear the good news, and let us hear it as Adam did—from the lips of God Himself. For that which is revealed for our belief is set before us on God's authority, not on man's. We are not only to believe the truth, but we are to believe it because God has spoken it. Faith must have a divine foundation.

We gather together a few of these *divine* announcements, asking the reader to study them as divine. Nor let him say that he knows them already; but let him accept our invitation to traverse, along with us, the field of gospel statement. It is of God Himself that we must learn; and it is only by listening to the very words of God that we shall arrive at the true knowledge of what the gospel is. His own words are the truest, the simplest, and the best. They are not only the most likely to meet our case; but they are the words that He has promised to honour and bless.

Let us hear, then, the words of God as to His own grace, or free-love, or mercy: 'The Lord passed by before him, and proclaimed, The Lord, The LORD GOD, *merciful and gracious, long-suffering*, and *abundant in goodness* and truth, keeping *mercy* for thousands, *forgiving iniquity and transgression and sin*' (Exod. 34:6-7). 'The Lord is *long-suffering*, and of *great mercy*' (Num. 14:18). 'His *mercies* are *great* ' (2 Sam. 24:14). 'The Lord your God is *gracious and merciful* (2 Chron. 30:9). 'Thou art a God *ready to pardon, gracious and merciful* ' (Neh. 9:17). 'His *mercy endureth for ever* (1 Chron 16:34). 'Thou, Lord, art *good*, and *ready to forgive*; and *plenteous in mercy* unto all them that call upon thee' (Ps. 86:5). 'Thou, O Lord, art a God *full of compassion*, and *gracious, long-suffering*, and *plenteous in mercy* and truth' (Ps. 86:15). 'Thy *mercy* is great unto the heavens' (Ps. 57:10). 'Thy *mercy* is great above the heavens' (Ps. 108:4). 'His *tender mercies* are over all his works' (Ps. 145:9).

'Who is a God like unto thee, that *pardoneth iniquity,* and passeth by the transgression of the remnant of his heritage? he retaineth not his anger for ever, because he *delighteth in mercy*' (Micah 7:18). '*I will love* them *freely*' (Hos. 14:4). 'God so *loved* the world, that he gave his only begotten Son' (John 3:16). 'God commendeth his *love* toward us' (Rom. 5:8). 'God, who is *rich in mercy*, for *his great love wherewith he hath loved us*, even when we were dead in sins' (Eph. 2:4-5). 'The *kindness and love* of God our Saviour toward man' (Titus 3:4). 'According to his *mercy* he saved us' (Titus 3:5). 'In this was manifested the *love of God* toward us, because that God sent his only begotten Son into the world, that we might live through him. Herein is *love*, not that we loved God, but that *he loved* us, and sent his Son to be the propitiation for our sins' (1 John 4:9-10). 'The only begotten of the Father, *full of grace* and truth' (John 1:14). '*Grace* and truth came by Jesus Christ' (John 1:17); 'the word of his *grace*' (Acts 14:3); 'the gospel of the *grace* of God' (Acts 20:24).

Such are a few of the words of Him who cannot lie concerning His own grace, or free-love. These sayings are faithful and true; and though perhaps we may but little have owned them as such, or heeded the truth that they embody, yet they are fitted to speak peace to the soul even of the most troubled. Each of these words of grace is like a star sparkling in the blue sky above us; or like a well of water pouring out its freshness amid desert rocks and sands.

Let no one say, 'We know all these passages; of what use is it to read and re-read words so familiar?' Of great use! Chiefly because it is in such declarations regarding the riches of God's free-love that the gospel is wrapped up; and it is out of these that the Holy Spirit ministers light and peace to us. Such are the words that He delights to honour as His messengers of joy to the soul. Hear then, in these, the voice of the Spirit's love, as well as the love of the Father and the Son! If you find no peace coming out of them to you as you read them the first time, read them again. If you find nothing the second time, read them once more. If you find nothing the hundredth or the thousandth time, study them yet again. 'The word of God is quick [i.e., living], and powerful' (Heb. 4:12); His sayings are the 'lively oracles' (Acts 7:38); His Word 'liveth and abideth for ever' (1 Pet. 1:23); it is 'like as a fire...and like a hammer that breaketh the rock in pieces' (Jer. 23:29). The gospel is 'the power of God' (Rom. 1:16); and it is 'by manifestation of the truth' that we commend ourselves to every man's conscience in the sight of God (2 Cor. 4:2).

There are no words like those of God, in heaven or in earth. Hence it is that you are to study 'that which is written'; for He Himself wrote it, and He wrote it for you. Do not think it needless to read these passages again and again. They will blaze up at last, and light up that dark soul of yours with the very joy of heaven.

You have sometimes looked up to the sky at twilight, searching for a star that you expected to find in its usual place. You did not see it at first, but you knew it was there, and that its light was undiminished. So instead of closing your eye or turning away to some other object, you continued to gaze more and more intently on the spot where you knew it was. Slowly and faintly the star seemed to come out in the sky as you gazed; and your persevering search ended in the discovery of the long-sought gem.

Just so it is with those passages that speak to you of the free-love of God. You say, I have looked into them, but they contain nothing for me. Do not turn away from them, as if you knew them so well already that you could find nothing new in them. You have not seen them yet. There are wonders beyond all price, hidden in each one. Take them up again. Search and study them. The Holy Spirit is most willing to reveal to you the glory that they contain. It is His office, it is His delight to be the sinner's Teacher. He will not be behind you in willingness. It is of the utmost moment that you should remember, this lest you should grieve and repel Him by your distrust.

Never lose sight of this great truth that the evil thing in you, which is the root of bitterness to the soul, is distrust of God; distrust of the Father, who so loved the world as to give His Son; distrust of the Son, who came to seek and save that which was lost; distrust of the Holy Ghost, whose tender mercies are over you and whose work of love is to reveal the Christ of God to your souls.

Besides, keep this in mind, that, in teaching you, He is honouring His own Word and glorifying Christ. You need not then suspect Him of indifference toward you, or doubt His willingness to enlighten 'the eyes of your understanding' (Eph. 1:18). While you are firmly persuaded that it is only *His* teaching that can be of any real use to you, do not grieve Him by separating His love in writing the Bible for you, from His willingness to make you understand it. He who gave you the Word will interpret it for you. He does not stand aloof from you or from His own Word, as if He needed to be persuaded, or bribed by your deeds and prayers, to unfold the heavenly truth to you. Trust Him for teaching. Avail yourself at once of His love and power. Do not say, I am not entitled to trust Him till I am converted. You are to trust Him *as a sinner*, not as a converted man. You are to trust Him as you are, not as you hope to be made before long. Your conversion is not your warrant for trusting Him.

The great sin of an unconverted man is his not trusting the God that made him, Father, Son, and Spirit—and how can anyone be so foolish, not to say wicked, as to ask for a warrant for forsaking sin? What would you say to a thief who said, I have no warrant to forsake stealing; I must wait till I am made an honest man, then I shall give it up? And what shall I say to a distruster of God who tells me that he has no warrant for giving up his distrust, for he is not entitled to trust God till he is converted? One of the greatest things in conversion is turning from distrust to trust. If you are not entitled to turn at once from distrust to trust, then your distrust is not sin. If, however, your distrust of the Holy Spirit be one of your worst sins, how absurd it is to say, I am not entitled to trust Him till I am converted!—for is not that just saying, I am not entitled to trust Him till I trust Him?

You say that you know God is gracious; yet, by your acting, you show that you do not believe Him to be so—or, at least, to be so gracious as to be willing to show you the meaning of His own Word. You believe Him to be so gracious as to give His only begotten Son; yet the way in which you treat Him, as to His Word, shows that you do not believe He is willing to give His Spirit to make known His truth. You think yourself much more willing to be taught than He is to teach, more willing to be blessed than He is to bless.

You say, I must wait till God enlightens my mind. If God had told you that waiting is the way to light, you would be right. But He has nowhere told you to wait; your idea of waiting is a mere excuse for not trusting Him immediately. If your way of proceeding be correct, God must have said both 'Come', and 'Wait'; 'Come now, but do not come now', which is a contradiction.

When a kind rich man sends a message to a poor cripple to come at once to him and be provided for, he sends his carriage to convey him. He does not say, 'Come; but then, as you are lame, and have besides no means of conveyance, you must use all the means in your power to induce me to send my carriage for you.' The invitation and the carriage go together.

Much more is this true of God and His messages. His Word and His Spirit go together. Not that the Spirit is *in* the Word, or the power *in* the message, as some foolishly tell you. They are distinct things, but they go together. And your mistake lies in supposing that He who sent the one may not be willing to send the other. You think that it is He, not yourself, who creates the interval which you call 'waiting'—although this waiting is, in reality, a deliberate refusal to comply with a command of God, and a determination to do something else that He has not commanded instead; a determination to make the doing of that something else an excuse for not doing the very thing commanded! Thus it is that you rid yourself of blame by pleading inability; in fact, you throw the blame on God for not being willing to do immediately that which He is most willing to do.

God demands immediate acceptance of His Son, and immediate belief of His gospel. You evade this duty on the plea that, as you cannot accept Christ of yourself, you must go and ask Him to enable you to do so. By this pretext, you try to relieve yourself from the overwhelming sense of the necessity for immediate obedience. You soothe your conscience with the idea that you are doing what you can, in the meantime, and that thus you are not so guilty of unbelief as before, seeing you *desire* to believe, and are doing *your* part in this great business!

It will not do. The command is, 'Believe on the Lord Jesus Christ.' Nothing less than this is pleasing to God. And though it is every man's duty to pray, just as it is every man's duty to love God and to keep His statutes, yet you must not delude yourself with the idea that you are doing the right thing when you only pray to believe, instead of believing. The thief may desire to give up stealing, and pray to be enabled to give it up; yet he is still a thief until he actually gives it up.

The question is not as to whether prayer is a duty, but whether it is a right and acceptable thing to pray *in unbelief.* It is every man's duty to pray; and it is absurd, as it is unscriptural, to say that a man's being unconverted releases him from this duty. But the real point that we press home upon the sinner is this: Is it to believing or unbelieving prayer that God is calling you? Unbelieving prayer is prayer to an unknown God, and it cannot be your duty to pray to an unknown God.

You must get on your knees, believing either that God is willing, or that He is not willing, to bless you. In the latter case, you cannot expect any answer or blessing. In the former case, you are really, though unconsciously, believing already; as it is written, 'He that cometh to God must believe that he is, and that he is a rewarder of them that diligently seek him' (Heb. 11:6). In maintaining the duty of praying before believing, you cannot surely be asserting that it is your duty to go to God in unbelief? Are you to persist in unbelief till, in some miraculous way, faith drops into you, and God compels you to believe? Must you go to God with unacceptable prayer, in order to induce Him to give you the power of acceptable prayer? Is this what you mean by the duty of praying in order to believe? If so, it is a delusion and a sin.

Understanding prayer in the scriptural sense, I would tell every man to pray, just as I would tell every man to believe—for prayer includes and presupposes faith. It assumes that the man knows something of the God he is going to, and that is faith. 'Whosoever shall call upon the name of the Lord shall be saved' (Rom. 10:13). But then the apostle adds, 'How then shall they call on him in whom they have not believed?' (v. 14). Does not this last verse go to the very root of the matter before us? It is every man's duty to 'call on the name of the Lord' (Joel 2:32; Acts 2:21); indeed, it is the great sin of the ungodly that they do not do so (Ps. 14:4; Jer. 10:25). Yet says the apostle, 'How shall they call on him in whom they have not believed?'

But I do not enter further on this point here. It may come up again. Meanwhile, I would just remind you concerning God's free-love in the free gift of His Son. Listen to what He Himself has told you regarding this, and know the God who is asking you to call upon His name—for if you but knew this God and His great gift of love, you would ask of Him and He would give you living water (John 4:10). Remember that the gospel is not a list of duties to be performed, or feelings to be produced, or a frame of mind that we are to pray ourselves into, in order to make God think well of us and to fit us for receiving pardon. The gospel is the good news of the great work done upon the cross. The knowledge of that finished work is immediate peace.

Read again and again the wonderful words that I have quoted at length from His own Book. The Bible is a living Book, not a dead one; a divine one, not a human one; a perfect one, not an imperfect one.[1] Search it, study it, dig into it. My son, says God, our Father, receive My words; hide My commandments with thee; incline thine ear unto wisdom; take fast hold of instruction; attend unto My wisdom and bow thine ear to My understanding; keep My words and lay up My commandments with thee.

Do not say these messages are only for the children of God; for, as if to prevent this, God thus speaks to the 'simple', the 'scorners', the 'fools': 'Turn ye at my reproof' (Prov. 1:23)—showing us that it is in listening to His words that the simple, the scorner, and the fool cease to be such, and become sons. Do not revert to the old difficulty about your need of the Holy Spirit; for, as if to meet this, God, in the above passage, adds, 'Behold, I will pour out

---

1   'We must make a great difference between God's word and the word of man. A man's word is a little sound which flieth into the air and soon vanisheth; but the word of God is greater than heaven and earth, yea, it is greater than death and hell, for it is the power of God, and remaineth everlastingly. Therefore we ought diligently to learn God's word, and we must know certainly and believe that God himself speaketh with us' (Luther).

my Spirit unto you, I will make known my words unto you.'
Not for one moment would God allow you to suspect His
willingness to accompany His Word with His Spirit.

Honour the words of God, and honour Him who wrote
them, by trusting Him for interpretation and light. Do not
disparage them by calling them 'a dead letter'. They are
not dead. If you will use the figure of 'death' in this case,
use it rightly. They are 'the savour of death unto death in
them that perish'; but this only shows their vitality. As the
blood of Christ either cleanses or condemns, so the words
of the Spirit either kill or make alive.

Again I say to you, honour the words of God. Make much
of them. 'Them that honour me I will honour' (1 Sam.
2:30), is as true of Scripture as it is of the God of Scripture.
Peace, light, comfort, life, salvation, [and] holiness are
wrapped up in them. 'Thy word hath quickened me' (Ps.
119:50). 'I will never forget thy precepts: for with them
thou hast quickened me' (v. 93).

It is through 'belief of the truth…[that] God hath from
the beginning chosen [us] to salvation' (2 Thess. 2:13). It is
'with the word of truth' that He begets us (James 1:18), and
all this is in perfect harmony with the great truth of man's
total helplessness and his need of the almighty Spirit.

'So then faith cometh by hearing, and hearing by the
word of God' (Rom. 10:17). 'Hear, and your soul shall live'
(Isa. 55:3).

8

BELIEVE AND BE SAVED

It is the Holy Spirit alone that can draw us to the cross and fasten us to the Saviour. He who thinks he can do without the Spirit has yet to learn his own sinfulness and helplessness. The gospel would be no good news to the dead in sin, if it did not tell of the love and power of the divine Spirit as explicitly as it announces the love and power of the divine Substitute.

But, while keeping this in mind, we may try to learn from Scripture what is written concerning the bond that connects us individually with the cross of Christ, thereby making us partakers of the pardon and the life which that cross reveals.

Thus, then, it is written, 'By grace are ye saved through faith; and that not of yourselves: it is the gift of God' (Eph. 2:8).

Faith, then, is the link, the one link, between the sinner and the Sin-bearer. It is not faith as a work or exercise of our minds, which must be properly performed in order to qualify or fit us for pardon. It is not faith as a religious duty, which must be gone through according to certain rules in order to induce Christ to give us the benefits of His work. It is faith simply as a receiver of the divine record concerning the Son of God. It is not faith considered as the source of holiness, as containing in itself the seed of all spiritual excellence and good works. It is faith alone, recognising simply the completeness of the great sacrifice for sin, and the trueness of the Father's testimony to that completeness—as Paul writes to the Thessalonians, 'our testimony among you was believed' (2 Thess. 1:10). It is not faith as a piece of money or a thing of merit; but faith taking God at His word, and giving Him credit for speaking the honest truth when He declares that 'Christ died for the ungodly' (Rom. 5:6), and that the life which that death contains for sinners is to be had 'without money and without price' (Isa. 55:1).

But let us learn about this faith from the lips of God Himself. I lay great stress on this in dealing with inquirers. For the more that we can fix the sinner's eye and conscience upon God's own words, the more likely shall we be to lead him aright, and to secure the quickening presence of that almighty Spirit who alone can give sight to the blind. One great difficulty which the inquirer finds is that of unlearning much of his past experience and teaching. Hence the importance of studying the divine words themselves, by which the sinner is made wise unto salvation. For they both unteach the false and imperfect, and teach the true and the perfect.

Let us see how frequently and strongly God has spoken respecting 'faith' and 'believing'. 'Without faith it is impossible to please [God]' (Heb 11:6). 'Therein is the righteousness of God revealed from faith to faith: as it is written, The just shall live by faith' (Rom. 1:17). 'The righteousness of God which is by faith of Jesus Christ unto all and upon all them that believe' (Rom. 3:22). 'Whom God hath set forth to be a propitiation through faith in his blood...to declare his righteousness...that he might be just, and the justifier of him which believeth in Jesus' (Rom. 3:25-26). 'He that believeth...shall be saved' (Mark 16:16). 'As many as received him, to them gave he power to become the sons of God, even to them that believe on his name' (John 1:12).

'And as Moses lifted up the serpent in the wilderness, even so must the Son of man be lifted up: That whosoever believeth in him should not perish, but have eternal life. For God so loved the world, that he gave his only begotten Son, that whosoever believeth in him should not perish, but have everlasting life. For God sent not his Son into the world to condemn the world; but that the world through him might be saved. He that believeth on him is not condemned: but he that believeth not is condemned already, because he hath not believed in the name of the only begotten Son of God' (John 3:14-18). 'He that believeth on the Son hath everlasting life: and he that believeth not the Son shall not see life' (John 3:36). 'He that heareth my word, and believeth on him that sent me, hath everlasting life' (John 5:24). 'This is the work of God, that ye believe on him whom he hath sent' (John 6:29). 'He that believeth on me shall never thirst' (John 6:35).

'This is the will of him that sent me, that every one which seeth the Son, and believeth on him, may have everlasting life' (John 6:40). 'He that believeth in me, though he were dead, yet shall he live: and whosoever liveth and believeth in me shall never die' (John 11:25-26). 'I am come a light into the world, that whosoever believeth on me should not abide in darkness' (John 12:46). 'These are written, that ye might believe that Jesus is the Christ, the Son of God; and that believing ye might have life through his name' (John 20:31). 'By him all that believe are justified from all things' (Acts 13:39). 'Believe on the Lord Jesus Christ, and thou shalt be saved' (Acts 16:31). 'To him give all the prophets witness, that through his name whosoever believeth in him shall receive remission of sins' (Acts 10:43). 'To him that worketh not, but believeth on him that justifieth the ungodly, his faith is counted for righteousness' (Rom. 4:5). 'Christ is the end of the law for righteousness to every one that believeth' (Rom. 10:4). 'If thou shalt confess with thy mouth the Lord Jesus, and shalt believe in thine heart that God hath raised him from the dead, thou shalt be saved' (Rom. 10:9). 'It pleased God by the foolishness of preaching to save them that believe' (1 Cor. 1:21). 'This is his commandment, that we should believe on the name of his Son Jesus Christ' (1 John 3:23). 'We have known and believed the love that God hath to us' (1 John 4:16).

'Whosoever believeth that Jesus is the Christ is born of God' (1 John 5:1). 'He that believeth on the Son of God hath the witness in himself: he that believeth not God hath made him a liar; because he believeth not the record that God gave of his Son' (1 John 5:10). 'He that believeth not shall be damned' (Mark 16:16).

These are some of the many texts that teach us what the link is between the sinner and the great salvation. They show that it is our belief of God's testimony concerning His own free-love and the work of His Son, that makes us partakers of the blessings which that testimony reveals. They do not ascribe any meritorious or saving virtue to our act of faith. They show us that it is the object of faith—the person, thing, or truth of which faith lays hold—that is the soul's peace and consolation. But still they announce most solemnly the necessity of believing, and the greatness of the sin of unbelief.

In [these verses] God demands the immediate faith of all who hear His testimony. Yet He gives no countenance to the self-righteousness of those who are trying to perform the act of faith in order to qualify themselves for the favour of God—whose religion consists in performing acts of faith of a certain kind, whose comfort arises from thinking of these well-performed acts, and whose assurance comes from the summing up of these at certain times and dwelling upon the superior quality of many of them.

In some places the word trust occurs where perhaps we might have expected faith. But the reason of this is plain:

the testimony that faith receives is testimony to a person and his good-will, in which case belief of the testimony and confidence in the person are things inseparable. Our reception of God's testimony is confidence in God Himself and in Jesus Christ His Son. Hence it is that Scripture speaks of 'trust' or 'confidence' as that which saves us, as if it would say to the sinner, 'Such is the gracious character of God that you have only to put your case into His hands, however bad it be, and entrust your soul to His keeping, and you shall be saved.'

In some places, we are said to be saved by the knowledge of God or of Christ; that is, by simply knowing God as He has made Himself known to us in Jesus Christ (Isa. 53:11; 1 Tim. 2:4; 2 Pet. 2:20). Thus Jesus spoke, 'This is life eternal, that they might know thee the only true God, and Jesus Christ, whom thou hast sent' (John 17:3). And, as if to make simplicity more simple, the apostle, in speaking of the facts of Christ's death, burial, and resurrection, says, 'By which also ye are saved, if ye keep in memory what I preached unto you' (1 Cor. 15:1-2).

Thus God connects salvation with 'believing', 'trusting', 'knowing', 'remembering'. Yet the salvation is not in our act of believing, trusting, knowing, or remembering; it is in the thing or person believed on, trusted, known, [and] remembered. Nor is salvation given as a reward for believing and knowing. The things believed and known are our salvation. Nor are we saved or comforted by thinking about our act of believing, or ascertaining that it possesses all the proper ingredients and qualities which would induce God to approve of it, and of us because of it. This would be making faith a meritorious, or, at least, a qualifying work—and then grace would be no more grace. It would really be making our faith a part of Christ's work—the finishing stroke put to the great undertaking of the Son of God, which otherwise would have been incomplete, or at least unsuitable for the sinner as a sinner.

To the man that makes his faith and his trust his rest, and tries to pacify his conscience by getting up evidence of their solidity and excellence, we say, miserable comforters are they all (Job 16:2)! I get light by using my eyes, not by thinking about my use of them, nor by a scientific analysis of their component parts. So I get peace by and in believing, not by thinking about my faith, or trying to prove to myself how well I have performed the believing act. We might as well extract water from the desert sands as peace from our own act of faith. Believing in the Lord Jesus Christ will do everything for us; believing in our own faith, or trusting in our own trust, will do nothing.

Thus faith is the bond between us and the Son of God; and it is so, not because of anything in itself, but because it is only through the medium of truth, as known and believed, that the soul can get hold of things or persons. Faith is nothing, save as it lays hold of Christ; and it does so by laying hold of the truth or testimony concerning Him. 'Faith cometh by hearing, and hearing by the word of God', says the apostle. 'Ye shall know the truth', says the Lord, 'and the truth shall make you free' (John 8:32); and again, 'Because I tell you the truth, ye believe me not...And if I say the truth, why do ye not believe me?' (John 8:45-46).

We have also such expressions as these: Those 'which believe and know the truth' (1 Tim. 4:3); those that 'do not obey the truth' (Rom. 2:8); 'as the truth is in Jesus' (Eph. 4:21); 'belief of the truth' (2 Thess. 2:13); 'acknowledging of the truth' (2 Tim. 2:25); 'the way of truth' (2 Pet. 2:2); 'we are of the truth' (1 John 3:19); 'sanctify them through thy truth' (John 17:17); I 'speak forth the words of truth' (Acts 26:25); 'the Spirit of truth...will guide you into all truth' (John 16:13).

Most memorable, in connection with this subject, are the Lord's warnings in the parable of the sower, especially the following: 'The seed is the word of God. Those by the way side are they that hear; then cometh the devil, and taketh away the word out of their hearts, lest they should believe and be saved' (Luke 8:11-12). The words, too, of the beloved disciple are no less so: 'He that saw it bare record, and his record is true: and he knoweth that he saith true, that ye might believe' (John 19:35); and again, 'These are written, that ye might believe that Jesus is the Christ, the Son of God; and that believing ye might have life through his name' (John 20:31).[1]

---

1   In this matter there are (as in most Bible statements) *two sides*— both to be held fast—belief *in* a *person*, and belief *of* a *truth*. The former, carried to an exclusive excess, lands us in mysticism; the latter, carried to a like extreme, ends in rationalism. We must realise both the person and the truth.

This truth regarding Christ and His sacrificial work, the natural man hates, because he hates Christ Himself. 'They hated me', says the Lord (John 15:25); even more, they hated me 'without a cause' (Ps. 69:4). It is not error that man hates, but truth; and hence the necessity for the Holy Spirit's work to remove that hatred; to make the sinner even so much as willing to know the truth or the True One. Yet there is no backwardness on the part of God to give the Spirit. The first dawnings of inquiry and anxiety show that something beyond 'flesh and blood' is at work in the soul.

But though it needs the power of the divine Spirit to make us believing men, this is not because faith is a mysterious thing, a great exercise or effort of soul, which must be very accurately gone through in order to make it and us acceptable; but because of our dislike to the truth believed, and our enmity to the Being in whom we are asked to confide. Believing is the simplest of all mental processes; yet, not the less is the power of God needed. Let not the inquirer mystify or magnify faith in order to give it merit or importance in itself, so that by its superior texture of quality it may justify him; yet, on the other hand, never let him try to simplify it for the purpose of making the Spirit's work unnecessary. The more simple that he sees it to be, the more will he see his own guilt, in so deliberately refusing to believe, and his need of the divine Helper to overcome the fearful opposition of the natural heart to the simple reception of the truth.

The difficulty of believing has its real root in pure self-righteousness; and the struggles to believe of which men speak, the endeavours to trust, are the indications and expressions of this self-righteousness. So far are these spiritual exercises from being tokens for good, they are often mere expressions of spiritual pride, evidences of the desperate strength of self-righteousness—the very earnestness of the struggle showing the intensity of the self-righteousness. It is worse than vain, then, to try to comfort an anxious soul by pointing to these efforts as proofs of existing faith. They are proofs either of ignorance or of unbelief—proofs of the sinner's determination to do anything rather than believe that all is done. Doubts are not the best evidence of faith; and attempts at performing this great thing called faith are more proofs of blindness to the finished propitiation of the Son of God.

To do some great thing called faith in order to win God's favour, the sinner has no objection; in fact it is just what he wants, for it gives him the opportunity of working for his salvation. But he rejects the idea of taking his stand upon a work already done and so ceasing his own efforts to effect a reconciliation, for which all that is needed was accomplished nineteen hundred years ago upon the cross of Him who was 'made...sin for us, who he knew no sin; that we might be made the righteousness of God in him' (2 Cor. 5:21).

9

BELIEVE JUST NOW

You are in earnest now; but I fear you are making your earnestness your Christ, and actually using it as a reason for not trusting Christ *immediately.* You think your earnestness will lead on to faith, if it be but sufficiently intense and long enough persisted in.

But there is such a thing as earnestness in the wrong direction: earnestness in unbelief, and a substitution of earnestness for simple faith in Jesus. You must not soothe the alarms of conscience by this earnestness of yours. It is unbelieving earnestness, and that will not do. What God demands is simple faith in the record that He has given you of His Son. You say, I can't offer Him faith, but I can bring Him earnestness; and by giving Him earnestness, I hope to persuade Him to give me faith. This is self-righteousness! It shows that you regard both faith and earnestness as something to be done in order to please God and secure His good-will. You say, Faith is the gift of God, but earnestness is not. It is in my own power; therefore I will earnestly labour, struggle, and pray, hoping that before long God will take pity on my earnest struggles. You even feel secretly that it would be hardly fair in Him to disregard such earnestness.

Now, if God has anywhere said that unbelieving earnestness or the unbelieving use of means is the way of procuring faith, I cannot object to such proceedings on your part. But I do not find that He has said so, or that the apostles, in dealing with inquirers, set them upon this preliminary process for acquiring faith. I find that the apostles shut up their hearers to *immediate faith and repentance*, bringing them face to face with the great object of faith, and commanding them in the name of the living God to believe—just as Jesus commanded the man with the withered hand to stretch it out. The Lord did not give him any directions as to a preliminary work, or preparatory efforts, struggles, and using of means.

These are man's attempts to bridge over the great gulf of human appliances; man's way of evading the awful question of his own *utter impotence.* [These are] man's unscriptural devices for sliding out of inability into ability, out of unbelief into faith; man's plan for helping God to save him. [These are] man's self-made ladder for climbing up a little way out of the horrible pit, in the hope that God will so commiserate his earnest struggles as to do all the rest that is needed.

Now God has commanded all men everywhere to repent (Acts 17:30); but He has nowhere given us any directions for obtaining repentance. God has commanded sinners to believe, but He has not prescribed for them any preparatory process, the undergoing of which will induce Him to give them something that He is not from the first most willing to do. It is thus that He shuts them up to faith by concluding 'them all in unbelief ' (Rom. 11:32). It is thus that He brings them to feel both the greatness and the guilt of their inability; and so constrains them to give up every hope of doing anything to save themselves, driving them out of every refuge of lies—and showing them that these prolonged efforts of theirs are hindrances, not helps; and are just so many rejections of His own immediate help, so many distrustful attempts to persuade Him to do what He is already most willing to do in their behalf.

The great manifestation of self-righteousness is this struggle to believe. Believing is not a *work*, but a ceasing from work; and this struggle to believe is just the sinner's attempt to make a work out of that which is no work at all, to make a labour out of that which is a resting from labour. Sinners will not let go their hold of their former confidences, and drop into Christ's arms. Why? Because they still trust these confidences, and do not trust Him who speaks to them in the gospel. Instead, therefore, of encouraging you to exert more and more earnestly these preliminary efforts, I tell you they are all the sad indications of self-righteousness. They take for granted that Christ has not done His work sufficiently, and that God is not willing to give you faith till you have plied Him with the arguments and importunities of months or years.

God is at this moment willing to bless you; and these struggles of yours are not, as you fancy, humble attempts on your part to take the blessing, but proud attempts either to put it from you, or to get hold of it in some way of your own. You cannot, with all your struggles, make the Holy Spirit more willing to give you faith than He is at this moment. But your self-righteousness rejects this precious truth; and if I were to encourage you in these 'efforts', I should be fostering your self-righteousness and your rejection of this grace of the Spirit.

You say you cannot change your heart or do any good thing. So say I. But I say more. I say that you are not at all aware of the extent of your helplessness and of your guilt. These are far greater and far worse than you suppose. And it is your imperfect view of these that leads you to resort to these endeavours. You are not yet sensible of your weakness, in spite of all you say. It is this that is keeping you from God, and God from you.

God commands you to believe and to repent. It is at your peril that you attempt to alter this imperative and immediate obligation by the substitution of something preliminary—the performance of which may perhaps soothe your terrors, and lull your conscience to sleep, but will not avail either to propitiate God or to lift you into a safer or more salvable condition, as you imagine. For we are saved by *faith*, not by efforts to induce 'an unwilling God' to give us faith. In going to God, we are to take for granted that He will fulfil His Word, and act according to His character. Our appeals are to be made, not to an unwilling, but to a willing God. We are not to try by our prayers or earnestness to persuade God to be gracious, to extort salvation from the hand of a grudging and austere giver. God is pressing His salvation upon us, and declaring His infinite willingness to bless at this moment.

God *commands* you to believe; and so long as you do not believe, you are making Him a liar, you are rejecting the truth, you are believing a lie—for unbelief is, in reality, the belief of a lie. Yes, God commands you to believe, and your not believing is your worst sin—and it is by exhibiting it as your worst sin that God shuts you up to faith. Now, if you try to extenuate this sin—if you flatter your soul that, by making all these earnest and laborious efforts to believe, you are lessening this awful sin and rendering your unbelieving state a less guilty one—then you are deluding your conscience, and thrusting away from you that divine hand which, by this conviction of unbelief, is shutting you up to faith.

I do not remember having seen this better stated than in Fuller's *Gospel Worthy of All Acceptation.* I give a few sentences:

> It is the duty of ministers not only to exhort their carnal hearers to believe in Jesus Christ for the salvation of their souls; but it is at our peril to exhort them to anything short of it, or which does not involve or imply it. We have sunk into such a compromising way of dealing with the unconverted, as to have well nigh lost sight of the spirit of the primitive preachers; and hence it is that sinners of every description can

sit so quietly as they do in our places of worship. Christ and His apostles, without any hesitation, called on sinners to repent and believe the gospel; but we, considering them as poor, impotent, and depraved creatures, have been disposed to drop this part of the Christian ministry. Considering such things as beyond the power of their hearers, they seem to have contented themselves with pressing on them the things they could perform, [while] still continuing as enemies of Christ—such as behaving decently in society, reading the Scriptures, and attending the means of grace.

Thus it is that hearers of this description sit at ease in our congregations. But as this implies no guilt on their part, they sit unconcerned, conceiving that all that is required of them is to lie in the way and wait the Lord's time. But is this the religion of the Scriptures? Where does it appear that the prophets or apostles treated that kind of inability, which is merely the effect of reigning aversion, as affording any excuse? And where have they descended in their exhortations to things that might be done, and the parties still continue the enemies of God? Instead of leaving out everything of a spiritual nature, because their hearers could not find it in their hearts to comply with it, it may be safely affirmed that they exhorted to nothing else, treating such inability not only as of no account with regard to the lessening of obligation, but as rendering the subjects of it worthy of the severest rebuke...

Repentance toward God and faith toward our Lord Jesus Christ are allowed to be duties, but not *immediate* duties. The sinner is considered as unable to comply with them, and therefore they are not urged upon him; but instead of them, he is directed to pray for the Holy Spirit to enable him to repent and believe. This, it seems, he *can* do, notwithstanding the aversion of his heart from everything of the kind! But if any man be required to pray for the Holy Spirit, it must be either sincerely and in the name of Jesus, or insincerely and in some other way. The latter, I suppose, will be allowed to be an abomination in the sight of God; he cannot, therefore, be required to do this; and as to the former, it is just as difficult and as opposite to the carnal heart as repentance and faith themselves. Indeed, it amounts to the same thing; for a sincere desire after a spiritual blessing, presented in the name of Jesus, is no other than the prayer of faith.

The great thing which I would press upon your conscience is the *awful guilt* that there is in unbelief. Continuance in unbelief is continuance in the very worst of sins; and continuance in it because (as you say) you cannot help it, is the worst aggravation of your sin. The habitual drunkard says he 'cannot help it'; the habitual swearer says he 'cannot help it'; the habitual unbeliever says he 'cannot help it'. Do you admit the drunkard's excuse? Or do you not tell him that it is the worst feature of his case, and that he ought to be utterly ashamed of himself for using such a plea? Do you say, I know you can't give up your drunken habits, but you can go and pray to God to enable you to give up these habits, and perhaps God will hear you and enable you to do so? What would this be but to tell him to go on drinking and praying alternately; and that, possibly, God may hear his drunken prayers, and give him sobriety? You would not thus deal with drunkenness; ought you to deal so with unbelief? Ought you not to press home its guilt; and to show a sinner that, when he says 'I can't help my unbelief', he is uttering his worst condemnation, and saying, 'I can't help distrusting God, I can't help hating God, I can't help making God a liar'—and that he might just as well say, 'I can't help stealing, lying, and swearing'.

Never let unbelief be spoken of as a *misfortune*. It is awfully sinful. Its root is the desperate wickedness of the heart. How evil must that heart be when it will not even believe! If our helplessness and hardness of heart lessened our guilt, then the more wicked we became, we should be the less responsible and the less guilty. The sinner who loves sin so much that he 'cannot' part with it is the most guilty. He who says, 'I cannot love God', is proclaiming himself one of the worst of sinners; but he who says, 'I cannot even believe', is taking to himself a guilt that we may truly call the darkest and most damnable of all.

Oh, the unutterable guilt involved even in one moment's unbelief, one single act of an unbelieving soul! How much more is the continuous unbelief of twenty or sixty years! To steal once is bad enough. How much more to be a thief by habit and repute! We think it bad enough when a man is overtaken with drunkenness; how much more when we have to say of him, 'he is never sober'. Such is our charge against the man who has not yet known Christ. He is a *continuous* unbeliever. His life is one unbroken course of unbelief—and hence of false worship, if he worships at all.[1] Every new moment is a new act of unbelief; a new commission of the worst of sins; a sin in comparison with

---

1   There is a tendency among some to undervalue doctrine, to exact morality at the expense of theology, and to deny the importance of a sound creed. I do not doubt that a sound creed has often covered an unsound life, and that much creed, little faith, is true of multitudes. But when we hear it said, 'Such a man is far gone in error, but his heart is in its right place; he disbelieves the substitution on the cross, but he rests on Christ Himself'—we wonder, and ask, What then was the Bible written for? It may be (if this be the case) a book of thought like Bacon's *Novum Organum*, but it is no standard of truth, no infallible expression of the mind of an infallible being! The solemnity with which that book affirms the oneness of truth, and the awful severity with which it condemns every departure from the truth, as a direct attack on God Himself, show us the danger of saying that a man's heart may be in its right place though his head contains a creed or error. Faith and unbelief are not mere mental manipulations, to which no moral value is attached. Doctrine is not a mere form of thought or phase of opinion. Within what limits such might have been the case had there been no revelation, I do not say. But, with a revelation, all mental transactions as to truth and error assume a moral character, with which the highest responsibility is connected; their results have a moral value, and are linked with consequences of the most momentous kind. On true doctrine rests the worship of the true God. If, then, Jehovah is a jealous God, not giving His glory to another, unbelief must be one of the worst of sins; and error not only a deadly poison to the soul receiving it, but hateful to God as blasphemy against Himself, and the same in nature as the blind theologies of paganism, on which is built the worship of Baal, or Brahm, or Jupiter. The real root of all unbelief is atheism. Man's guilty conscience modifies this, turns it into idolatry; or his sentimental nature modifies it,

which all other sins both of heart and life, awful as they are, seem to lose their enormity.

Let the thought of this guilt cut your conscience to the quick! Oh, tremble as you think of what it is to be—not for a day or an hour, but for a whole lifetime—an unbelieving man!

and turns it into pantheism. The fool's 'No God' is really the root of all unbelief.

10

The Want of Power to Believe

You say, I know all these things, yet they bring me no peace.

I doubt much, in that case, whether you do know them; and I should like you to begin to doubt upon this point. You take for granted much too easily that you know them. Seeing they do not bring to your soul the peace that God says they are *sure* to do, your wisest way would be to suspect the correctness of your knowledge. If a trusted physician prescribes a sure medicine for some complaint, and if on trial I find that what I have taken does me no good, I begin to suspect that I have got some wrong medicine instead of that which he prescribed.

Now, are you sure that the truth which you say you know is the very gospel of the grace of God? Or is it only something like it? And may not the reason of your getting no peace from that which you believe just be because it contains none? You have got hold of many of the good things, but you have missed, perhaps, the one thing that made it a 'joyful sound' (Ps. 89:15). You believe, perhaps, the whole gospel save the one thing that makes it good news to a sinner. You see the cross as bringing salvation very near; but not so absolutely close as to be in actual contact with you as you are; not so entirely close but that there is a little space, just a handbreadth or a hairbreadth, to be made up by your own prayers, efforts, or feelings. 'Everything', you say, 'is complete; but that want of feeling in myself!' Ah, there it is! There is the little unfinished bit of Christ's work that *you* are trying to finish, or to persuade Him by your prayers to finish for you! That want of feeling is the little inch of distance which you have to get removed, before the completeness of Christ's work is available for you!

The consciousness of insensibility, like the sense of guilt, ought to be one of your reasons for trusting Him the more, whereas you make it a reason for not trusting Him at all. Would a child treat a father or a mother thus? Would it make its bodily weakness a reason for distrusting parental love? Would it not feel that that weakness was thoroughly known to the parent, and was just the very thing that was drawing out more love and skill? A stronger child would need less care and tenderness. But the poor, helpless one would be of all others the most likely to be pitied and watched over. Deal thus with Christ, and make that hardness of heart an additional reason for trusting Him, and for prizing His finished work.

This state of mind shows that you are not believing the right thing, but something else, which will not heal your hurt; or, at least, that you are mixing up something with the right thing, which will neutralise all its healing properties.

You must begin at the beginning once more; and go back to the simplest elements of heavenly truth, which are wrapped up in the great facts that 'Jesus died and rose again' (1 Thess. 4:14); facts too little understood and undervalued by many; facts to which the apostles attached such vast importance and on which they laid so much stress; facts out of which the early believers, without the delay of weeks or months, extracted their peace and joy.

You say, 'I cannot believe.' Let us look into this complaint of yours. I know that the Holy Spirit is as indispensable to your believing, as is Christ in order to your being pardoned. The Holy Spirit's work is direct and powerful; and you will not rid yourself of your difficulties by trying to persuade yourself that His operations are all indirect, and merely those of a teacher presenting truth to you. Salvation *for* the sinner is Christ's work; salvation *in* the sinner is the Spirit's work. Of this internal salvation He is the beginner and the ender. He works in you in order to your believing, as truly as He works in you after you have believed, and in consequence of your believing.

This doctrine, instead of being a discouragement, is one of unspeakable encouragement to the sinner; and he will acknowledge this if he knows himself to be the thoroughly helpless being that the Bible says he is. If he is not totally depraved, he will feel the doctrine of the Spirit's work a hindrance and an insult, no doubt—just as an able-bodied traveller would feel that you were both hindering and insulting him, if you were to tell him that he cannot set out on his journey without taking your arm. But as, in that case, he will be able to save himself without much assistance, he might just set aside the Spirit altogether, and work his way to heaven alone!

The truth is that without the Spirit's direct and almighty help, there could be no hope for a totally depraved being at all.

You speak of this inability to believe as if it were some unprovided for difficulty; and as if the discovery of it had greatly cast you down. You would not have been so despondent had you found that you could believe of yourself without the Spirit; and it would greatly relieve you to be told that you could dispense with the Spirit's help in this matter. If this would relieve you, it is plain that you have no confidence in the Spirit; and you wish to have the power in your own hands because you believe your own willingness to be much greater than His. Did you but know the blessed truth that His willingness far exceeds yours, you would rejoice that the power was in His hands rather than in your own. You would feel far more certain of attaining the end desired, when the strength needed is in hands so infinitely gracious; and you would feel that the man who told you that you had all the needed strength in yourself was casting down your best hope, and robbing you of a heavenly treasure.

How eagerly some grasp at the idea that they *can* believe, and repent, and turn of themselves, as if it were consolation to the troubled spirit! As if this were the unravelling of its dark perplexities! Is it comfort to persuade yourself that you are not wholly without strength? Can you, by lessening the sum total of your depravity and inability, find the way to peace? Is it a relief to your burdened spirit to be delivered from the necessity of being wholly indebted to the Spirit of God for faith and repentance? Will it rescue you from the bitterness of despair to be told that, though you have not enough strength left to enable you to love God, yet in virtue of some little remaining power, you can perform this least of all religious acts: believing on the Son of God?

If such be your feeling, it is evident that you do not know the extent of your own disease, nor the depths of your evil heart. You don't understand the good news brought to you by the Son of God—of complete deliverance from all that oppresses you, whether it be guilt or helplessness. You have forgotten the blessed announcement, 'In the Lord have I righteousness and *strength*' (Isa. 45:24). Your strength, as well as your righteousness, is in another; yet, while you admit the former, you deny the latter. You have forgotten, too, the apostle's rejoicing in the strength of his Lord; his feeling that when he was weak, then he was strong; and his determination to glory in his infirmities, that the power of Christ might rest upon him (2 Cor. 12:9).

If you understand the genuine gospel in all its freeness, you will feel that the man who tries to persuade you that you have strength enough left to do without the Spirit, is as great an enemy of the cross and of your soul, as the man who wants to make you believe that you are not altogether guilty, but have some remaining goodness—and therefore do not need to be wholly indebted for pardon to the blood and righteousness of Immanuel.

'Without strength' is as literal a description of your state as 'without goodness'. If you understood the gospel, the consciousness of your total helplessness would just be the discovery that you are the very sinner to whom the great salvation is sent; that your inability was all foreseen and provided for, and that you are in the very position which needs, which calls for, and which shall receive, the aid of the almighty Spirit.

Till you feel yourself in this extremity of weakness, you are not in a condition (if I may say so) to receive the heavenly help. Your idea of remaining *ability* is the very thing that repels the help of the Spirit, just as any idea of remaining goodness thrusts away the propitiation of the Saviour. It is your not seeing that you have no strength that is keeping you from believing. So long as you think you have some strength, you will be trying to use that strength in *doing* something—and specially in performing, to your own and Satan's satisfaction, that great act or exercise of soul called 'faith'. But when you find out that you have no strength left, you will, in despair, cease to work—and (before you are aware) believe! For, if believing be not a ceasing from work, it is at least the necessary and immediate result of it. You expended your little stock of imagined strength in holding fast the ropes of self-righteousness; but now, when the conviction of having no strength at all is forced upon you, you drop into the arms of Jesus. But this you will never do as long as you fancy that you have strength to believe.

Paul, after many years' believing, still drew his strength from Christ alone; how much more must you and others who have never yet believed at all? *He* said, 'I take pleasure in my infirmities', that is, my want of strength. *You* say, I am cast down because of it!

They who tell you that you have some power left, and that you are to use that power in believing and repenting, are enemies of your peace and subverters of the gospel. They in fact say to you that faith is a work, and that you are to do that work in order to be saved. They mock you. In yielding to them, you are maintaining that posture which vexes and resists the Spirit, who is striving within you. You are proudly asserting for fallen man a strength that belongs only to the unfallen. You are denying the completeness of the divine provision made for the sinner, in the fullness of Him in whom it pleased the Father that all fullness should dwell.

The following passage from an old writer is worth pondering:

> Ask him what it is he finds [that] makes believing difficult to him. Is it unwillingness to be justified and saved? Is it unwillingness to be so saved by Jesus Christ, to the praise of God's grace in him, and to the voiding of all boasting in himself? This he will surely deny. Is it a distrust of the truth of the gospel record? This he dare not own. Is it a doubt of Christ's ability or

good-will to save? This is to contradict the testimony of God in the gospel. Is it because he doubts of an interest in Christ and His redemption? You tell him that believing on Christ makes up the interest in him. If he says that he cannot believe on Jesus Christ because of the difficulty of the acting this faith, and that a divine power is needful to draw it forth, which he finds not—you tell him that believing in Jesus Christ is no work, but a resting on Jesus Christ; and that this pretence is as unreasonable as that if a man wearied with a journey, and who is not able to go one step farther, should argue, 'I am so tired that I am not able to lie down,' when, indeed, he can neither stand nor go. The poor wearied sinner can never believe on Jesus Christ till he finds he can do nothing for himself, and in his first believing doth always apply himself to Christ for salvation, as a man hopeless and helpless in himself. And by such reasonings with him from the gospel, the Lord will (as He has often done) convey faith, joy, and peace by believing.

Your puzzling yourself with this 'cannot' shows that you are proceeding in a wrong direction. You are still labouring under the idea that this believing is a work to be done by you, and not the simple acknowledgment of a work done by another. You would do something in order to get peace, and you think that if you could only do this great thing called faith, God would reward you with peace. In this view, faith is a price as well as a work—whereas it is neither, but a ceasing from work and from attempting to pay for salvation. Faith is not a climbing of the mountain, but a ceasing to attempt it, and allowing Christ to carry you up in His arms.

You seem to think that it is your own *act* of faith that is to save you; whereas it is the *object* of your faith, without which your own act of faith, however well performed, is nothing. Supposing that this believing is a mighty work, you ask, 'How am I to get it properly performed?' But your peace is not to come from any such performance, but entirely from Him to whom the Father is pointing: 'Behold my servant, whom I have chosen' (Matt. 12:18). As if He would say, 'Look at Him as Israel looked at the serpent of brass: forget everything about yourself; your faith, your feelings, your repentance, your prayers; and look at Him.' It is in Him, and not in your poor act of faith, that salvation lies. It is in Him and in His boundless love that you are to find your resting place. It is out of Him, not out of your exercise of soul concerning Him, that peace is to come. Looking at your own faith will only minister to your self-righteousness.

To seek for satisfaction as to the *quality* or *quantity* of your faith, before you will take comfort from Christ's work, is to proceed upon the supposition that that work is not sufficient of itself to give you comfort as soon as received; that until made sufficient by a certain amount of religious feeling, it contains no comfort to the sinner. In short, that the comforting ingredient is an indescribable something, depending for its efficiency chiefly upon the superior excellence of your own act of faith, and the success of your own exertions in putting it forth.

Your inability, then, is not of performing aright this great act of believing, but of ceasing from all such self-righteous attempts to perform any act, or *do* anything whatever, in order to your being saved. So that the real truth is that you have not yet seen such a sufficiency in the one great work of the Son of God upon the cross, as to lead you utterly to discontinue your wretched efforts to work out something of your own. As soon as the Holy Spirit shows you the entire sufficiency of the great propitiation of the sinner, *just as he is*, you cease your attempts to act or work; and take, instead of all such exercises of yours, that which Christ has done. The Spirit's work is not to enable a man to *do* something that will save him or help to save him, but so to detach him from all his own exertions and performances, whether good, bad, or indifferent, that he shall be content with the salvation which the Saviour of the lost has finished.

Remember, that what you call your inability, God calls your guilt; and that this inability is a *wilful* thing. It was not put into you by God, for He made you with the full power of doing everything He tells you to do. You disobey and disbelieve willingly. No one forces you to do either. Your rejection of Christ is the free and deliberate choice of your own will.

That inability of yours is a fearfully wicked thing. It is the summing up of your depravity. It makes you more like the devil than almost anything else, incapable of loving God, or even of believing on His Son! Capable only of hating Him, and of rejecting Christ! O dreadful guilt! Unutterable wickedness of the human heart!

Is it really the 'cannot' that is keeping you back from Christ? No; it is the 'will not'. You have not got the length of the 'cannot'. It is the 'will not' that is the real and present barrier. 'Ye *will not* come to me, that ye might have life' (John 5:40). 'Whosoever *will*, let him take the water of life freely' (Rev. 22:17).

If your heart would speak out, it would say, 'Well, after all, I cannot, and God will not. I am doing all I can to believe, but the Spirit will not help me.' And what is this but saying, 'I have a hard-hearted God to deal with, who will not help or pity me.' Whatever your rebellious heart may say, Christ's words are true: 'Ye *will* not.'

What He spoke, when weeping over impenitent Jerusalem, He speaks to you, '*I would...*and *ye would not*' (Matt. 23:37). 'They are fearful words', writes Dr Owen,[1] '"*ye would not.*" Whatever is pretended, it is will and stubbornness that lie at the bottom of this refusal.' And oh! what must be the strength as well as the guilt of this unbelief, when nothing but the almightiness of the Holy Ghost can root it out of you!

You are perplexed by the doctrine of God's sovereignty and election. I wonder that any man believing in a God should stumble at these. For if there be a God—a 'King, eternal, immortal, and invisible' (1 Tim. 1:17)—He cannot but be sovereign, and He cannot but do according to His

---

1   John Owen (1616-1683).

own will and choose according to His own purpose. You may dislike these doctrines, but you can only get rid of them by denying altogether the existence of an infinitely wise, glorious, and powerful Being. God would not be God were He not thus absolutely sovereign in His present doings and His eternal pre-arrangements.

But how would it solve your perplexities to get rid of sovereignty and election? Suppose these were set aside, you still remain the same depraved and helpless being as before. The truth is, that the sinner's real difficulty lies neither in sovereignty nor election, but in *his own depravity*. If the removal of these 'hard doctrines' (as some call them) would lessen his own sinfulness, or make him more able to believe and repent, the hardship would lie at their door; but if not, then these doctrines are no hindrance at all. If it be God's sovereignty that is keeping him from coming to Christ, the sinner has serious matter of complaint against the doctrine. But if it be his own depravity, is it not foolish to be objecting to a truth that has never thrown one single straw of hindrance in the way of his return to God?[2]

---

2 Yet let me notice a way of speaking of this sovereignty which is not scriptural. Some tell the anxious sinner that the first thing he has to do, in order to faith, is to submit to this sovereignty, and that when he has done so, God will give him faith! This is far wrong surely. Submission to the divine sovereignty is one of the highest results of faith—how can it be preparatory to faith? The sinner is told that he cannot believe of himself, but he can submit himself to God's sovereignty! He cannot do the lowest thing, but he can do the highest—nay, and he must begin by doing the highest, in order to prepare himself for doing the lowest! It is faith, not unbelief, that will thus submit; and yet the unconverted

Election has helped many a soul to heaven, but never yet hindered one. Depravity is the hindrance; election is God's way of overcoming that hindrance. And if that hindrance is not overcome in all, but only in some, who shall find fault? Was God bound to overcome it in all? Was He bound to bring every man to Christ and to pluck every brand from the burning? Do not blame God for that which belongs solely to yourself, nor fret and be troubled about His sovereignty when the real root of the evil is your own desperately wicked heart.

---

sinner is recommended to do, and to do in unbelief, the highest act of faith! This surely is turning theology upside down.

11

INSENSIBILITY

You say that you do not *feel* yourself to be a sinner: that you are not 'anxious' enough, that you are not 'penitent' enough. Be it so. Let me, however, ask you such questions as the following:

1. *Does your want of feeling alter the gospel?* Does it make the good news less free, less suitable? Is [the gospel] not glad tidings of God's love to the unworthy, the unlovable, the *insensible*? Your not feeling your burdens does not affect the nature of the gospel, nor change the gracious character of Him from whom it comes. It suits you as you are, and you suit it exactly. It comes up to you on the spot and says, Here is a whole Christ for you; a Christ containing everything you need. Remember the invitation: it is to him 'that hath no money' (Isa. 55:1). Is not this just your state? Your acquisition of feeling would not qualify you for it, nor bring it nearer, nor buy its blessings, nor make you

more welcome, nor persuade God to do anything for you, that He is not at this moment most willing to do.

2. *Is your want of feeling an excuse for your unbelief?* Faith does not spring out of feeling, but feeling out of faith. The less you feel, the more you should trust. You cannot feel aright till you have believed. As all true repentance has its root in faith, so all true feeling has the same. It is vain for you to attempt to reverse God's order of things.

3. *Is your want of feeling a reason for your staying away from Christ?* A sense of want should lead you to Christ and not keep you away. 'More are drawn to Christ', says old Thomas Shephard, 'under a sense of a dead, blind heart, than by all sorrows, humiliations, and terrors'. The less of feeling or conviction that you have, the more needy you are; and is that a reason for keeping aloof from Him? Instead of being less fit for coming, you are more fit. The blindness of Bartimaeus was his reason for coming to Christ, not for staying away (Mark 10:46). If you have more blindness and deadness than others, you have so many more reasons for coming, so many fewer for standing far off. Whatever others may do who have convictions, you who have none dare not stay away, nor even wait an hour. You must come!

4. *Will your want of feeling make you less welcome to Christ?* How is this? What makes you think so? Has He said so, or did He act, when on earth, as if this were

His rule of procedure? Had the woman of Sychar any feeling when He spoke to her so lovingly? (John 4:10).

Was it the amount of conviction in Zacchaeus that made the Lord address him so graciously? The balm will not be the less suitable for you, nor the physician the less affectionate and cordial, because, in addition to other diseases, you are afflicted with the benumbing palsy. Your greater need only gives Him an opportunity of showing the extent of His fulness as well as the riches of His grace. Come to Him, then, just because you do not feel. 'Him that cometh to me I will in no wise cast out' (John 6:37). Whatever you may feel, or may not feel, it is still 'a faithful saying, and worthy of all acceptation, that Christ Jesus came into the world to save sinners'. Do not limit the grace of God, nor suspect the love of Christ. Confidence in that grace and love will do everything for you; want of confidence, nothing. Christ wants you to come—not to wait, nor to stay away.

5. *Will your remaining away from Christ remove your want of feeling*? No. It will only make it worse; for it is a disease that He only can remove, so that a double necessity is laid upon you for going to Him. Others who feel more than you may linger; you cannot afford to do so. You must go immediately to Him, who is 'a Prince and a Saviour, for to give repentance to Israel, and forgiveness of sins' (Acts 5:31). Seeing that distance and distrust will do nothing for you, try what 'drawing near' and 'confidence' will do. To you, though the

chief of sinners, the message is, 'Let us draw near' (Heb. 10:22).

God commands you to come without any further delay or preparation; to bring with you your sins, your unbelief, your insensibility, your heart, your will, your whole man, and to put them into Christ's hands. God demands your immediate confidence and instant surrender to Christ. 'Kiss the Son' is His message (Ps. 2:12). His Word insists on your return: 'Return unto the Lord thy God' (Hosea 14:1). It shows you that the real cause of the continuance of this distance is your unwillingness to let Christ save you in His own way, and a desire to have the credit of removing your insensibility by your own prayers and tears.

6. *Is not your insensibility one of your worst sins?* A hard-hearted child is one of the most hateful of beings. You may pity and excuse many things, but not hard-heartedness. Cease then to pity yourself, and learn only to condemn. Give this sin no quarter. Treat it not as a misfortune, but as unmingled guiltiness. You may call it a disease, but remember that it is an inexcusable *sin*. It is one great all-pervading sin added to your innumerable others. This should shut you up to Christ. As an incurable leper, you must go to Him for cure. As a desperate criminal, you must go to Him for pardon. Do not, I beseech you, add to this awful sin the yet more damning sin of refusing to acknowledge Christ as the Healer of all diseases, and the Forgiver of all iniquities.

Repentance is only to be got from Christ. Why then should you make the want of it a reason for staying away from Him? Go to Him for it. He is exalted to give it. If you speak of 'waiting', you only show that you are not sincere in your desire to have it. No man in such circumstances would think of waiting. Your conviction of sin is to come not by *waiting* but by *looking*—looking to Him whom your sins have crucified, and whom by your distrust and unbelief you are crucifying afresh. It is written, 'They shall look on me whom they have pierced, and they shall mourn' (Zech. 12:10). It is not, they shall 'mourn and look', but they shall 'look and mourn'.

Beware of fancying that convictions are to save you, or that they are to be desired for their own sakes. Thus writes an old minister, 'I was put out of conceit with legal terrors; for I thought they were good, and only esteemed them happy that were under them; they came, but I found they did me ill; and unless the Lord had guided me thus, I think I should have died doting after them.' And another says, 'Sense of a dead, hard heart is an effectual means to draw to Christ; yea, more effectual than any other can be, because it is the poor, the blind, the naked, the miserable, that are invited.'

As to what is called a 'law-work', preparatory to faith in Christ, let us consult the Acts of the Apostles. There we have the preaching of the apostolic gospel, and the fruits of it in the conversion of thousands. We have several inspired sermons addressed both to Jew and Gentile; but into none of these is the Law introduced. That which pricked the hearts of the three thousand at Pentecost was a simple narrative of the life, death, burial, and resurrection of Jesus of Nazareth, concluding with these awful words, which must have sounded like the trumpet of doom to those who heard them, 'Therefore let all the house of Israel know assuredly, that God hath made that same Jesus, whom ye have crucified, both Lord and Christ' (Acts 2:36). These were words more terrible than law, more overwhelming than heard at Sinai. Awful as it would have been to be told, 'You have broken the whole Law of God'; it was not so awful as being told, 'You have crucified His Son!' The sin of crucifying the Lord of glory was greater than that of breaking a thousand laws. And yet in that very deed of consummate wickedness was contained the gospel of the grace of God. That which pronounced the sinner's condemnation declared also his deliverance. There was life in that death; the nails that fastened the Son of God to the cross, let out the pent-up stream of divine love upon the murderers themselves!

The gospel was the apostolic hammer for breaking hard hearts in pieces, for producing 'repentance unto life' (Acts 11:18). It was a believed gospel that melted the obduracy of the self-righteous Jew; and nothing but the good news of God's free love, condemning the sin yet pardoning the sinner, will in our own day melt the heart of stone. 'Law and terrors do but harden'; and their power, though wielded by an Elijah, is feeble in comparison with that of a preached cross.

The word *repentance* signifies in the Greek 'change of mind'; and the Holy Spirit produces this change in connection with the gospel, not the Law. 'Repent and believe the gospel' (Mark 1:15) does not mean, 'get repentance by the Law, and then believe the gospel'; but 'let this good news about the kingdom, which I am preaching, lead you to change your views and receive the gospel'. Repentance being put before faith here simply implies that there must be a turning from what is false in order to the reception of what is true. If I would turn my face to the north, I must turn it from the south; yet I should not think of calling the one of these preparatory to the other. If I want to get rid of the darkness, I must let in the light; but I should not say that the getting rid of the darkness is a preparation for receiving the light. These must, in the nature of things, go together. Repentance, then, is not, in any sense, a preliminary qualification for faith— least of all in the sense of sorrow for sin. 'It must be reckoned a settled point,' says Calvin, 'that repentance not only immediately follows upon faith, but springs out of it... They who think that repentance goes before faith, instead of flowing from or being produced by it, as fruit from a tree, have never understood its nature'.[1]

That terror of conscience may go before faith, I do not doubt. But such terror is very unlike biblical repentance; and its tendency is to draw men away from, not to, the cross. That sinners may be awakened by the thunders of

---

1   Calvin, *Institutes of the Christian Religion*, Book III, ch. 3, sect. 1.

Law, I know. But these alarms are not godly sorrow. They are not uncommon among unbelieving men, such as Ahab and Judas (1 Kings 16:30ff; Matt. 27:3). They will be heard with awful distinctness in hell, but they are not repentance. Sorrow for sin comes from 'apprehension of the mercy of God in Christ', from the sight of the cross and of the love that the cross reveals. The broken and the contrite heart (Ps. 51:17) is the result of our believing the glad tidings of God's free love. In so far as repentance means sorrow for sin, or a change of mind respecting sin, it is produced only by looking to the cross. In so far as it is a change of mind in reference to God or Christ, it is the same with believing the gospel.

Few things are more dangerous to the anxious soul than the endeavours to get convictions, terrors, and humiliations as preliminaries to believing the gospel. They who would tell a sinner that the reason of his not finding peace is that he is not anxious enough, nor convicted enough, nor humbled enough, are enemies to the cross of Christ. They who would inculcate a course of prayer, humiliation, self-examination, and dealing with the Law in order to believe in Christ, are teaching what is the very essence of popery; not the less poisonous and perilous because refined from Romish grossness, and administered under the name of [the] gospel.

Christ asks no preparation of any kind whatsoever, legal or evangelical, outward or inward, in the coming sinner. And he that will not come as he is, shall never be received at all. It is not 'exercised souls', nor 'penitent believers', nor 'well-humbled seekers', nor earnest 'users of the means', nor any of the better class of Adam's sons and daughters, but sinners, that Christ welcomes. He 'came not to call the righteous, but sinners to repentance' (Luke 5:32).

Spurious repentance, the product and expression of unbelief and self-righteousness, may be found previous to faith; just as all manner of evils abound in the soul before it believes. But when faith comes, it comes not as the result of this self-wrought repentance, but in spite of it; and this so-called repentance will be afterwards regarded by the believing soul, as one of those self-righteous efforts whose only tendency was to keep the sinner from the Saviour. They who call on 'penitent sinners' to believe, mistake both repentance and faith; and that which they teach is no glad tidings to the sinner. To the better class of sinners (if such there be) who have by laborious efforts got themselves sufficiently humbled, it may be glad tidings; but not to those who are 'without strength' (Rom. 5:6): the lost, the ungodly, the hard-hearted, the insensible, the lame, the blind, the halt, the maimed. 'It is not sound doctrine,' says Dr Colquhoun, 'to teach that Christ will receive none but the true penitent, or that none else is warranted to come by faith to him for salvation. The evil of that doctrine is that it sets needy sinners on spinning repentance, as it were, out of their own bowels, and on bringing it with them to Christ, instead of coming to him by faith to receive it from him. If none be invited but the true penitent, then impenitent sinners are not bound to come to Christ; and cannot be blamed for not coming.'[2]

12

Jesus Only

You say, 'I am not satisfied with the motives that have led me to seek Christ; they are selfish.' That is very likely. The feelings of a newly awakened sinner are not disinterested, neither can they be so.

You have gone in quest of salvation from a sense of danger, or fear of the wrath to come, or a desire to obtain the inheritance of glory. These are some of the motives by which you are actuated. How could it be otherwise? God made you with these fears and hopes; and He appeals to them in His Word. When He says, 'Turn ye, turn ye…for why will ye die?' (Ezek. 33:11), He is appealing to your fears. When He sets eternal life before you and the joys of an endless kingdom, He is appealing to your hopes. And when He presents these motives, He expects you to be moved by them. To act upon such motives, then, cannot be wrong. Indeed, not to act upon them would be to harden yourself against God's most solemn appeals.

'Knowing therefore the terror of the Lord, we persuade men' (2 Cor. 5:11), says Paul. It cannot be wrong to be influenced by this terror. 'The remnant were affrighted, and gave glory to the God of heaven' (Rev. 11:13). This surely was not wrong. The whole Bible is full of such motives, addressed to our hopes and fears.

When was it otherwise among the millions who have found life in Christ, who began in any other way, or started with a purely disinterested motive? Was it not thus that the jailor at Philippi began, when the earthquake shook his soul and called up before his conscience the everlasting woe? Was it not a sense of danger and a dread of wrath that made him ask, 'What must I do to be saved?' (Acts 16:30). And did the apostle rebuke him for this? Did he refuse to answer his anxious question because his motive was so selfish? No; he answered at once, 'Believe on the Lord Jesus Christ, and thou shalt be saved' (Acts 16:31).

There is nothing wrong in these motives. When my body is pained, it is not wrong to wish for relief. When overtaken by sickness, it is not wrong to send for a physician. You may call this selfishness, but it is a right and lawful selfishness, which He who made us what we are, and who gave us our instincts, expects us to act upon—and in acting on which, we may count upon His blessing, not His rebuke. It is not wrong to dread hell, to desire heaven, to flee from torments, to long for blessedness, to shun condemnation, and to desire pardon.[1] Let not Satan then ensnare you

---

1   It is not wrong to love God for what He has done for us. Not to do so, would be the very baseness of ingratitude. To love God

with such foolish thoughts, the tendency of which is to quench every serious desire under the pretext of its not being disinterested and perfect.

You think that, were you seeking salvation from a regard to the glory of God, you would be satisfied. But what does that mean but that, at the very first, even before you have come to Christ, you are to be actuated by the highest of all motives? He who has learned to seek God's glory is one who has *already* come to Christ; and he who has learned to do this entirely is no sinner at all, and, therefore, does not need Christ. To seek God's glory is a high attainment of faith; yet you want to be conscious of possessing it before you have got faith; nay, in order to your getting it! Is it possible that you can be deluding yourself with the idea that if you could only secure this qualification, you might confidently expect God to give you faith? This would be substituting your own zeal for His glory, in the room of the cross of Christ.

Do not keep back from Christ under the idea that you must come to Him in a disinterested frame, and from an unselfish motive. If you were right in this thing, who

---

purely for what He is, is by some spoken of as the highest kind of love, into which enters no element of self. It is not so. For in that case, you are actuated by the pleasure of loving; and this pleasure of loving an infinitely lovable and glorious Being, of necessity introduces self. Besides, to say that we are to love God solely for what He is, and not for what He had done, is to make ingratitude an essential element of pure love. David's love showed itself in not forgetting God's benefits. But this pure love soars beyond David's and finds it a duty to be unthankful, lest perchance some selfish element mingle itself with its superhuman, superangelic purity.

could be saved? You are to come as you are, with all your bad motives, whatever these may be. Take all your bad motives, add them to the number of your sins, and bring them to the altar where the great sacrifice is lying. Go to the mercy-seat. Tell the High Priest there, not what you desire to be, not what you ought to be, but what you are. Tell Him the honest truth as to your condition at this moment. Confess the impurity of your motives, all the evil that you feel or that you don't feel, your hard-heartedness, your blindness, your unteachableness. Confess everything without reserve. He wants you to come to Him exactly as you are, and not to cherish the vain thought that—by a little waiting, working, or praying—you can make yourself fit, or persuade Him to make you fit.[2]

'But I am not satisfied with my faith', you say. No, truly. Nor are you ever likely to be so. At least I should hope not. If you wait for this before you have peace, you will wait till life is done. It would appear that you want to believe in your

2   How reasonable, writes one, that we should just do that one small act which God requires of us, go and tell Him the truth. I used to go and say, Lord, I am a sinner, do have mercy on me; but as I did not feel all this, I began to see that I was taking a lie in my hand, trying to persuade the Almighty that I felt things which I did not feel. These prayers and confessions brought me no comfort, no answer, so at last I changed my tone, and began to tell the truth—Lord, I do not feel myself a sinner; I do not feel that I need mercy. Now, all was right; the sweetest reception, the most loving encouragements, the most refreshing answers, this confession of truth brought down from heaven. I did not get anything by declaring myself a sinner, for I felt it not; but I obtained everything by confessing that I did not see myself one.

own faith in order to obtain rest to your soul. The Bible does not say, 'Being satisfied about our faith, we have peace with God', but 'Being *justified* by faith, we have peace with God' (Rom. 5:1); and between these two things there is a great difference.

Satisfaction with Jesus and His work, not satisfaction with your own faith, is what God expects of you. 'I am satisfied with Christ', you say. Are you? Then you are a believing man; and what more do you wish? Is not satisfaction with Christ enough for you or for any sinner? And is not this the truest kind of faith? To be satisfied with Christ is faith in Christ. To be satisfied with His blood is faith in His blood. Do not bewilder yourself, nor allow others to bewilder you. Be assured that the very essence of faith is being satisfied with Christ and His sin-bearing work; ask no more questions about faith, but go on your way rejoicing, as one to whom Christ is all.

Remember the Baptist's words, 'He must increase, but I must decrease' (John 3:30). Self, in every form, must decrease; and Christ must increase. To become satisfied with your faith would look as if you were dissatisfied with Christ. The beginning, middle, and end of your course must be dissatisfaction with self and satisfaction with Christ. Be content to be satisfied with faith's glorious object, and let faith itself be forgotten. Faith, however perfect, has nothing to give you. It points you to Jesus. It bids you look away from itself to Him. It says, 'Christ is all.' It bids you look to Him who says, 'Look unto me'; who says, 'Fear not; I am the first and the last: I am he that

liveth, and was dead; and, behold, I am alive for evermore'
(Rev. 1:17-18).

If you were required to believe in your own faith, to
ascertain its quality, and to know that you are born again,
before you were warranted to trust in Jesus or to have
peace, you would certainly need to be satisfied with your
own faith. But you are not required to make good any
personal claim, save that you are a sinner; not that you
feel yourself to be one (that would open up an endless
metaphysical inquiry into your own feelings), but simply
that you are one. This you know upon God's authority and
learn from His Word; and on this you act, whether you feel
your sinfulness or not. The gospel needs no ascertaining
of anything about ourselves, save what is written in the
Bible and what is common to all Adam's children: that
we need a Saviour. It is upon this need that faith acts; it is
this need that faith presents at the throne of grace. The
question, then, is not: Am I satisfied with my faith? but:
Am I a needy sinner, and am I satisfied that in Christ there
is all I need?

You say, 'I am not satisfied with my love.' What! Did
you expect to be so? Is it your love to Christ, or His love to
you, that is to bring you peace? God's free love to sinners,
as such, is our resting place. There are two kinds of love in
God—His love of compassion to the unbelieving sinner,
and His love of delight and complacency to His believing
children. A father's love to a prodigal child is quite as sincere
as his love to his obedient, loving child at home, though it
be of a different kind. God cannot love you *as a believer*

till you are such. But He loves you as a poor sinner. And it is this love of His to the unloving and unlovable that affords the sinner his first resting place. This free love of God attracts and satisfies him. 'Herein is love, not that we loved God, but that he loved us' (1 John 4:10). 'We love him, because he first loved us' (1 John 4:19). 'God so loved the world, that he gave his only begotten Son' (John 3:16).

'I am not satisfied with my repentance', you say. It is well. What would you have thought of yourself had you been so? What pride and self-righteousness would it indicate, were you saying, 'I am satisfied with my repentance; it is of the proper quality and amount'? If satisfied with it, what would you do with it? Would you ground your peace upon it? Would you pacify your conscience with it? Would you go with it, instead of the blood, to a holy God? If not, what do you mean by the desire to be satisfied with repentance before having peace with God?

In short, you are not satisfied with any of your religious feelings, and it is well that you are not so; for if you were, you must have a very high idea of yourself, and a very low idea of what both Law and gospel expect of you. You are, no doubt, right in not being satisfied with the state of your feelings, but what has this to do with the great duty of immediately believing on the Son of God? If the gospel is nothing to you till you have got your feelings all set right, it is no gospel for the sinner at all. But this is its special fitness and glory, that it takes you up at the very point where you are at this moment, and brings you glad tidings in spite of your feelings being altogether wrong.

All these difficulties of yours have their root in the self-esteem of our natures, which makes us refuse to be counted altogether sinners, and which shrinks from going to God, save with some personal recommendation to make acceptance likely. Utter want of goodness is what we are slow to acknowledge. Give up these attempts to be satisfied with yourself in anything, great or small, faith, feeling, or action. The Holy Spirit's work in convincing you of sin is to make you dissatisfied with yourself, and will you pursue a course that can only grieve Him away? God can never be satisfied with you on account of any goodness about you; and why should you attempt to be satisfied with anything that will not satisfy Him?

There is but one thing with which He is entirely satisfied—the person and work of His only-begotten Son. It is with Him that He wants you to be satisfied, not with yourself. How much better would it be to take God's way at once, and be satisfied with Christ? Then would pardon and peace be given without delay. Then would the favour of God rest upon you. For God has declared that whoever is satisfied with Christ shall find favour with Him. His desire is that you should come to be at one with Him in this great thing. He asks nothing of you, save this. But with nothing else than this will He be content, nor will He receive you on any other footing, save that of one who has come to be satisfied with Christ, and with what Christ has done.

Surely all this is simple enough. Does it not exactly meet your case? Satisfaction with yourself, even could you get it, would do nothing for you. Satisfaction with Christ would do everything; for Christ is all. 'This is my beloved Son, in whom I am well pleased' (Matt. 17:5). Be pleased with Him in whom the Father is pleased, and all is well.

I suspect that some of those difficulties of yours arise from the secret idea that the gospel is just a sort of *modified law*, by keeping which you are to be saved. You know that the old Law is far above your reach, and that it condemns, but cannot save you. But you think, perhaps, that Christ came to make the Law easier, to lower its demands, to make it (as some say) an evangelical Law, with milder terms, suited to the sinner's weakness. That this is blasphemy a moment's thought will show you. For it means that the former Law was too strict; that is, it was not 'holy, and just, and good' (Rom. 7:12). It denies also Christ's words, that He 'came not to destroy but to fulfil' the Law (Matt. 5:17). God has but one Law, and it is perfect; its substance is love to God and man. A milder law must mean an imperfect one, a law that makes God's one Law unnecessary, a law that gives countenance to sin. Will obedience to an imperfect law save a breaker of the perfect Law? But faith does not make void the Law; it establishes it (Rom. 3:31).

It is by a perfect Law that we are saved; else it would be an unholy salvation. It is by a perfect Law, fulfilled in every 'jot and tittle', that we are saved; else it would be an unrighteous salvation. The Son of God has kept the Law for us; He has magnified it and made it honourable; and thus we have a holy and righteous salvation. Though above Law in Himself, He was made 'under the law' (Gal 4:4) for us; and by the vicarious law-keeping of His spotless life, as well as by endurance unto death of that Law's awful penalties, we are redeemed from the curse of the Law.

'Christ is the end [i.e., the fulfilling and exhausting] of the law for righteousness to every one that believeth' (Rom. 10:4). For Christ is not a helper, but a Saviour. He has not come to enable us to save ourselves by keeping a mitigated Law, but to keep the unmitigated Law in our room, that the Law might have no claim for penalty upon any sinner who will only consent to be indebted to the law-keeping and law-magnifying life and death of the divine Surety.

Other difficulties spring from confounding the work of the Spirit *in us* with that of Christ *for us*. These must be kept distinct; for the intermingling of them subverts both. Beware of overlooking either; or keeping them at a distance from each other. Though distinct, they go hand in hand, inseparably linked together—yet each having its own place and office. Your medicine and your physician are not the same, yet they go together. Christ is our medicine, the Spirit is your physician. Do not take the two works as if they were one compound work; nor build your peace upon some mystic gospel made up of a mixture of the two. Realise both, the outward and the inward, the objective and the subjective; Christ for us, the Holy Spirit in us.

As at the first, so to the last must this distinctiveness be observed, lest having found peace in believing, you lose it by not holding the beginning of your confidence steadfast to the end. 'When I begin to doubt,' writes one,

'I quiet my doubts by going back to the place where I got them first quieted; I go and get peace again where I got it at the beginning. I do not sit down gloomily to muse over my own faith or unbelief, but over the finished work of Immanuel. I don't try to reckon up my experiences, to prove that I once was a believer, but I believe again as I did before. I don't examine the evidence of the Spirit's work in me, but I think of the sure evidences that I have of Christ's work for me in His death, burial, and resurrection. This is the restoration of my peace. I had begun to look at other objects; I am now recalled from my wanderings to look at Jesus only.'[3]

---

3 'Thus the poor and sorrowful soul, instead of being at once led to the source of all good, is taught to make much more of the conflict of truth and falsehood within it as the pledge of God's love; and to picture to itself faith as a sort of passive quality, which sits amid the ruins of human nature, and keeps up what may be called a silent protest, or indulges a pensive meditation over its misery. And, indeed, faith this regarded, cannot do more, for while it acts, not to lead the soul to Christ, but to detain it from him, how can the soul but remain a prisoner? True faith is what may be called colourless, like air or water; it is but the medium through which the soul sees Christ, and the soul as little rests on it and contemplates it as the eye can see the air. When men, then, are bent on holding it, as it were, in their hands—curiously inspecting, analyzing, and so aiming at it—they are obliged to colour and thicken it [so] that it may be seen and touched. That is, they substitute for it something or other, a feeling, notion, sentiment, conviction, an act of reason, which they may hang over and dote upon. They rather aim at experiences within them, than at Him who is without them. Now, men who are acted on by news, good and bad, or sights beautiful or fearful, admire, rejoice, weep, or are pained, but are moved spontaneously, not with a direct consciousness of their emotion. So is it with faith

Some of your difficulties seem to arise from mixing up the natural and supernatural. Now the marvellous thing in conversion is that while all is supernatural (being the work of the Holy Ghost), all is also natural. You are, perhaps, expecting some miraculous descent of heavenly power and brightness into your soul; something apart from divine truth and from the working of man's powers of mind. You have been expecting faith to descend like an angel from heaven into your soul, and hope to be lighted up like a new star in your firmament. It is not so.

The Spirit's work is beyond nature, but it is not against nature. He displaces no faculty; He disturbs no mental process; He does violence to no part of our moral framework; He creates no new organ of thought or feeling. His office is to 'set all to rights' within you; so that you never feel so calm, so true, so real, so perfectly natural, so much yourself—as when He has taken possession of you in every part and filled your whole man with His heavenly joy. Never do you feel so perfectly free—less constrained and less mechanical—in all your faculties, as when He has brought 'into captivity every thought to the obedience of Christ' (2 Cor. 10:5). The heavenly life imparted is liberty and peace; it is the removal of bondage, darkness, and pain. So far from being a mechanical constraint, it is the removal of the iron chain with which guilt had bound us. It acts like an army of liberation to a downtrodden country, like the warm breath of spring to the frost-fettered tree. For

and other Christian graces. Bystanders see our minds; but our minds, if healthy, see but the objects that possess them.'

the entrance of true life, or living truth, into man's soul must be liberty, not bondage. 'The truth shall make you free' (John 8:32).

Other difficulties arise out of confused ideas as to the proper *order* of truth. Misplaced truth is sometimes more injurious than actual error. In our statements of doctrine, we are to have regard to God's order of things, as well as to the things themselves. If you would solve the simplest question in arithmetic, the figures must not only be the proper ones, but they must be placed in proper order. So it is with the doctrines of the Word of God. Some seem to fling them about in ill-assorted couples, or confused bundles, as if it mattered little to the hearer or reader what order was preserved, provided only certain truths were distinctly announced. Much trouble to the anxious person has arisen from this reckless confusion.

A gospel in which election is placed first is not the gospel of the apostles; though certainly a gospel in which election is denied is still less the apostolic gospel. The true gospel is neither that Christ died for the elect, nor that He died for the whole world; for the excellency of the gospel does not lie in its announcement of the numbers to be saved, but in its proclamation of the great propitiation itself.

Some who are supposed to be holding fast 'the form of sound words' (2 Tim. 1:13) present us with a mere dislocation of the gospel; the different truths being so jumbled that, while they may be all there, they produce no result. They so neutralise each other as to prevent the sinner extracting from them the good news that, when rightly put together, they most assuredly contain. If the verses of the Epistle to the Romans were transposed or jumbled together, would it [still] be the Epistle to the Romans, though every word were there? So if, in teaching the gospel, we do not begin at the beginning—if, for instance, we tell the sinner what he has to do, before we tell him what God has done; if we tell him to examine his own heart before we tell him to study the cross of Christ— we take out the whole gladness from the glad tidings, and preach 'another gospel' (Gal. 1:6).

Do we not often, too, study the Bible as if it were a book of law, and not the revelation of grace? We draw a cloud over it, and read it as a volume written by a hard master. A harsh tone is thus imparted to its words, and the *legal* element obscures the *evangelical*. We are slow to read it as a revelation of the love of the Father, Son, and Holy Ghost; as the book of grace, specially written for us by the Spirit of grace. The Law no doubt is in it, yet the Bible is not law, but gospel. As Mount Sinai rears its head—an isolated mass of hard, red granite, amid a thousand desert mountains of softer and less stern material—so does the Law stand in the Bible: a necessary part of it, but not the characteristic of it. [The Law] 'was added because of transgressions, till the seed should come' (Gal. 3:19). Yet have not our suspicious hearts darkened this Book of light? Do we not often read it as the proclamation of a command *to do*, instead of a declaration of what the love of God *has done*?

In going to God at first, are you to take for granted His willingness, or His unwillingness, to bless? Most seem to do the latter. They even defend themselves by saying that, if they knew they were converted, they would take His willingness for granted; but not being sure of this, they dare not do so! As if the gospel were not the revelation of His willingness to receive sinners as such!

How strange! We believe in Satan's willingness to tempt and to injure; but not in God's willingness to deliver and to save! We yield to our great enemy when he seduces into sin, and leads away from Christ and heaven; but we will not yield to our truest Friend when He draws us with the bands of love! We will not give God credit for speaking truly when He speaks in tender mercy and utters over the sinner the yearnings of His unfathomable pity. We listen as if His words were hollow, as if He did not mean what He says, as if His messages of grace—instead of being the most thoroughly sincere that ever fell on human ears—were mere words spoken as a matter of course.

There is nothing in the whole Bible to repel the sinner, and yet the sinner will not come! There is everything to draw and to win; yet the sinner stands aloof! Christ receives sinners, yet the sinner turns away! He yearns over them, weeps over them as over Jerusalem (Luke 13:34); yet the sinner is unmoved! The heavenly compassion is unavailing; the infinite long-suffering does not touch the stony heart, and the divine tears are thrown away. The Son of God stretches out His hands all the day long, but the outstretched hands are disregarded. All, all seems in vain to arrest the heedless, and to win back the wanderer.

Oh! the amount of divine love that has been expended upon this sad world, that has been brought to bear upon the needy sons of men! We sometimes almost doubt whether it be true or possible that God should lavish such love on such a world. But the cross is the precious memorial of [God's] love, and that saying stands unchangeable: 'God so loved the world, that he gave his only begotten Son' (John 3:16).

Sometimes, too, we say, What is the use of throwing away such love? Is not the earnestness of God disproportioned to the littleness of its object: man? It would be so were this life all; were there no eternity, no heaven, no hell, no endless gladness, and no everlasting woe. But with such a destiny as man's, with an eternity like that which is in store for him, can any amount of earnestness be too great? Can love or pity exceed their bounds? Can the joy or grief over a sinner saved or lost be exaggerated?

He whose infinite mind knows what heaven is, knows what its loss must be to an immortal being. Can He be too much in earnest about its gain?—He whose all-reaching foresight knows what hell is, in all its neverending anguish, sees far off and fathoms the horrors of the lost soul: its weeping and wailing and gnashing of teeth forever and forever, its horrible sense of condemnation and unmitigated woe, its cutting remorse, its too-late repentance, its hopeless sighs, its bitter memories of earth's sunny hours, with all the thousand sadnesses that go to make up the sum total of a lost eternity! Can He then pity too much? Can He yearn too tenderly over souls that are madly bent on flinging themselves into a doom like this? Can He use words too strong or too affectionate in warning them against such a darkness, such a devil, and such a hell; [and] in beseeching them to make sure of such a heaven as His?

In the minds of some, the idea prevails that sin quenches pity for the sinner in the heart of God. It is not so. That it shall do so hereafter, and that God will cease to pity the lost, is an awful truth. The lost soul's eternity will be an unpitied eternity of woe. But, meanwhile, God's hatred of the sin is not hatred of the sinner. Nay, the greatness of his sin seems rather to deepen than to lessen the divine compassion. At least we may say that the increasing misery which increasing sin entails calls into new intensity the paternal pity of 'the God of the spirits of all flesh' (Num. 16:22). It grieves Him at His heart (Gen. 6:6). The further the prodigal goes into the far country, the more do the yearnings of the father's heart go out after him in unfeigned compassion for the wretched wanderer—in his famine, nakedness, degradation, and hopeless grief.

No, sin does not quench the pitying love of God. The kindest words ever spoken to Israel were in the very height of their apostasy. The most gracious invitation ever uttered by the Lord was to Capernaum, Bethsaida, and Chorazin: 'Come unto me' (Matt. 11:28). The most loving message ever sent to a church was that to Laodicea, the worst of all the seven, 'Behold, I stand at the door, and knock' (Rev. 3:20). It was Jerusalem, in her extremity of guilt and unbelief, that drew forth the tears of the Son of God. No, sin does not extinguish the love of God to the sinner.

Many waters cannot quench it, nor can the floods drown it. From first to last, God pursues the sinner as he flies from Him; pursues him not in hatred, but in love; pursues him not to destroy, but to save.

'God is not a man, that he should lie' (Num. 23:19). He means what He says when He speaks in pity as truly as when He speaks in wrath. His words are not, like man's, random expressions or utterances of vague sentiment or highly wrought representations of feelings. His words are all true and real. You cannot exaggerate the genuine feeling that they contain; to understand them as figures is not only to convert them into unrealities, but to treat them as falsehoods. Let sinners take God's words *as they are*: the genuine expressions of the mind of that infinitely truthful Being who uses nothing but the words of 'truth and soberness' (Acts 26:25).

God is sovereign, but that sovereignty is not at war with grace. Nor does it lead to insincerity of speech, as some seem to think. Whether we can reconcile the sovereignty with the pity, it does not matter. Let us believe them both, because both are revealed. Nor let us resort to an explanation of the words of pity which would imply that they were not sincerely spoken; and that if a sinner took them too literally and too simply, he would be sorely disappointed—finding them at last delusive exaggerations, if not empty air.

When Christ was on earth, He received and blessed and healed everyone who came to Him. Divine sovereignty did not hamper divine love; nor did love interfere with sovereignty. Each had its own place. There was no conflict between them. Christ spoke truly when He said, 'No man can come to me, except the Father…draw him' (John 6:44); and He spoke as truly when He said, 'him that cometh to me I will in no wise cast out' (John 6:37).

Let us learn to treat God as not merely the holiest, but the most truthful, of all beings. Let the heedless sinner hear His truthful warnings and tremble, for they shall all be fulfilled. Let the anxious sinner listen to His truthful words of grace, and be at peace. We need to be told this. For there is in the minds of many a feeling of sad suspicion as to the sincerity of the divine utterances, and a tendency to evade their honest meaning—and this even among those who do not seem at all aware of such distrust. Let us do justice to the truthfulness of God.

'God is love' (1 John 4:16). Yes, *God is love.* Can such a God be suspected of insincerity in the declarations of His long-suffering, in His words of yearning compassion toward the most rebellious and impenitent of men? That there is such a thing as righteousness, that there is such a place as hell, that there are such beings as lost angels and lost men, we know to be awful certainties. But however terrible and however true these things may be, they cannot cast the slightest doubt upon the sincerity of the great oath that God has sworn before heaven and earth: that He has 'no pleasure in the death of the wicked'; nor in the least blunt the solemn edge of His gracious entreaty, '*Turn ye, turn ye, for why will ye die?*' (Ezek. 33:11).

God's Way of Holiness

of Holiness

Growing in Grace
by Walking with God

Horatius
Bonar

Foreword by Matt Boswell

ISBN 978-1-5271-0610-9

GOD'S WAY OF HOLINESS
GROWING IN GRACE BY WALKING WITH GOD
HORATIUS BONAR

From the preface by Matt Boswell:
In the companion work to his book *God's Way of Peace*, Horatius Bonar shows us that a life that has been saved is a life that is holy. The Spirit of God works in us to make us holy. The saving work of Christ on the cross has given us the victory over sin, but while we are on this earth we battle on. Read and be encouraged.

… I have long had a fondness for the works of Bonar: his prose is pellucid and always cuts to the chase. And this influential work on holiness is no exception. In his day this subject was a much-controverted one and this book was a much-needed response to what some were rejecting as outmoded and even unbiblical. With brevity and modernity of phrase, Bonar sets forth the classical, and truly biblical, perspective on sanctification. And as such, it is of tremendous value today, for ours is a day when the pursuit of holiness is not so much disputed as forgotten. So, read and follow in the holy paths laid out here!

Michael A. G. Haykin
Chair and Professor of Church History and
Director of The Andrew Fuller Center for Baptist Studies,
The Southern Baptist Theological Seminary, Louisville,
Kentucky

ISBN 978-1-5271-0469-3

Absolutely Basic

The Everlasting Righteousness & Regeneration

Horatius Bonar and J. C. Ryle

This book contains two parts. The first is an updated and abriged version of Horatius Bonar's book The Everlasting Righteousness, first published in 1874. Its central theme is the substitutionary work of Jesus Christ. Bonar shows that, in Jesus Christ, God has provided the only way to deal with the problem of our sin. Because Jesus is the perfect substitute, anyone who believes in him receives a legal pardon from God, and the perfect righteousness of Jesus becomes theirs. This truth has enormous consequences for believers, and Bonar explains some of them in this wonderful book.

The second part is an updated version of Regeneration by J. C. Ryle, about the new birth. Ryle addresses what it means to be born again, and what it looks like in the life of a Christian.

Bonar and Ryle are both nineteenth-century gospel-infused preachers whose sermons and writings seem timeless. These abbreviated and updated samples should prove soul enriching to whoever reads them. Timeless truths told in effective and engaging ways.

Derek W. H. Thomas

Senior Minister of Preaching and Teaching, First Presbyterian Church, Columbia, South Carolina

Christian Focus Publications

Our mission statement –

STAYING FAITHFUL

In dependence upon God we seek to impact the world through literature faithful to His infallible Word, the Bible. Our aim is to ensure that the Lord Jesus Christ is presented as the only hope to obtain forgiveness of sin, live a useful life and look forward to heaven with Him.

Our books are published in four imprints:

CHRISTIAN FOCUS

Popular works including biographies, commentaries, basic doctrine and Christian living.

CHRISTIAN HERITAGE

Books representing some of the best material from the rich heritage of the church.

MENTOR

Books written at a level suitable for Bible College and seminary students, pastors, and other serious readers. The imprint includes commentaries, doctrinal studies, examination of current issues and church history.

CF4•K

Children's books for quality Bible teaching and for all age groups: Sunday school curriculum, puzzle and activity books; personal and family devotional titles, biographies and inspirational stories – because you are never too young to know Jesus!

Christian Focus Publications Ltd,
Geanies House, Fearn, Ross-shire,
IV20 1TW, Scotland, United Kingdom.
www.christianfocus.com